# AN ANALYTICAL SURVEY OF THE FIFTEEN SINFONIAS (THREE-PART INVENTIONS) BY J. S. BACH

Theodore O. Johnson

UNIVERSITY
PRESS OF
AMERICA

LANHAM • NEW YORK • LONDON

Library of Congress Cataloging in Publication Data

Johnson, Theodore O.
   An analytical survey of the fifteen sinfonias
(three-part inventions) by J.S. Bach.

   Includes index.
   1. Bach, Johann Sebastian, 1685-1750.   Inventions,
harpsichord, BWV 787-801.   2. Canons, fugues, etc.
(Harpsichord)—Analysis, appreciation.   I. Title.
MT145.B14J56   1986       786.1'092'4       86-9091
ISBN 0-8191-5377-X (alk. paper)
ISBN 0-8191-5378-8 (pbk. : alk. paper)

TO HARRIET KOEHLER JOHNSON

# CONTENTS

# PREFACE

The fifteen *Sinfonias* by Johann Sebastian Bach, commonly referred to as *Three-Part Inventions*, today, were termed *Fantasies* in the *Little Clavier Book*, where they originally appeared in 1720, along with other works, including the fifteen *Two-Part Inventions*, which were termed *Preludes* in this book. They were created as instructional pieces for Bach's oldest son, Wilhelm Friedemann, and the terms *Sinfonias* and *Inventions* were applied by Bach, himself, when they were isolated into a separate work in 1723. The title page of this work bears an oft-quoted inscription revealing Bach's concern for both the performance and compositional aspects of music:

Upright Instruction
wherein the lovers of the clavier, and especially those desirous of learning, are shown a clear way not alone (1) to learn to play clearly in two voices, but also, after further progress, (2) to deal correctly and well with three *obbligato* parts; furthermore, at the same time not alone to have good *inventiones* [ideas], but to develop the same well, and above all to arrive at a singing style in playing and at the same time to acquire a strong foretaste of composition.[1]

The *Inventions* and *Sinfonias*, which is to say, then, respectively, the *Two-Part Inventions* and *Three-Part Inventions*, employ keys that match on an item-by-item basis, starting with C major (Number One), continuing upward, and concluding with B minor (Number Fifteen). The C-Major Invention and those inventions based upon keys closely related to C major were composed first: D minor,

[1]Hans T. David and Arthur Mendel, *The Bach Reader* (New York, W. W. Norton & Company, 1966), p. 86.

vii

E minor, F major, G major, and A minor--in other words, with tonics moving right up the white keys of the keyboard, from C. B minor (up one more white key) is next, after which a descending order is observed: Bb major, A major, G minor, F minor, E major, Eb major, D major, and C minor. Altogether, nine of the twelve tones are represented as keynotes in the *Inventions* and *Sinfonias*, six of these--on the first six white notes (C, D, E, F, G, and A)--generating both major- *and* minor-key pieces; two, on Eb and Bb, major-key pieces only; and one, on B, a minor-key piece only. Therefore, none of these pieces goes beyond four sharps and four flats in its key signature, a feature which tends to limit the degree of playing difficulty. The *Well-Tempered Clavier*, on the other hand, has two volumes, each of which employs *all* twelve tones as keynotes for both major- and minor-key preludes and fugues.

The success of almost any piece of music hinges, at least in part, around its thematic basis, and the individual sinfonias are certainly no exception, especially because of their remarkable economy of means. Like the *Inventions*, the *Sinfonias* include certain pieces based upon brief germinating ideas often identified as *motives*, and other pieces based upon longer ideas best identified as *subjects*; those inventions and sinfonias which share the same keys, however, do not always correspond in terms of the use of a motive or subject, and, in fact, the longest subjects found in the *Sinfonias* are exceeded in length by the longest ones of the *Inventions*, a condition which may relate to the opportunity for additional imitation, and thus an automatically more substantial opening exposition, because of the third voice in the *Sinfonias*. Both the *Inventions and Sinfonias* contain certain subjects which are longer than some of the subjects found in the fugues of the *Well-Tempered Clavier*.

Some thematic resemblances exist between corresponding items from the *Inventions* and *Sinfonias*, as, for example, with the two subjects in B minor, or with the E-Major Sinfonia's subject and the E-Major Invention's initial countersubject fragment; however, striking similarities occur with certain *non*-corresponding items, such as the C-Minor Sinfonia subject's second half and the D-Minor Invention's entire subject (in transposition). One interior passage from the G-Minor Sinfonia (measures 36-41) also sounds very much like another interior passage from the A-Major Invention (measures 7-9 or 16-18). Similarity in *treatment* of material between corresponding items is sometimes apparent, as with both Bb-major pieces, which employ overlapping imitation in the form of canon and/or stretto.

Occasionally, the precise length or exact cut-off point of a subject or motive is in doubt (Sinfonias Three, Twelve, and Thirteen), but usually it is safe to presume that it ends just as its imitation is beginning.

One of the principal features distinguishing the sinfonia from the typical *Well-Tempered Clavier* three-voice fugue has to do with the opening texture, which is one-voice (monophonic) in the fugue and two-voice in the sinfonia, for the *Sinfonias* invariably employ a statement of the subject or motive in one of the upper voice-parts (the uppermost, *except* in Numbers Six, Eight, Nine, and Fourteen) accompanied by a contrapuntal line in the lowest voice-part, which (except in Number Five) begins directly *on* the first beat of the first measure, usually slightly before the subject or motive, which, in turn, frequently begins with*in* the first beat. Another point of difference between the sinfonia and the fugue concerns the voicing, which sometimes involves the lowest voice as the one initiating the subject in the fugue, but *never* does in the sinfonia, although in Number Fifteen, the lowest voice-part does provide the *second* entry for the only time. (Voice-parts, from top to bottom, are usually referred to as "soprano," "alto," and "bass," respectively, in this book.)

Economy of means does not preclude the use of a countersubject (or countermotive), a countersubject being a melodic idea associated with the subject or answer in a recurrent manner. All fifteen sinfonias have *some* such recurrence, but in certain ones (for example, Number Fourteen) it is exceedingly minimal, whereas in others (such as Number Three) it is extensive. Inventions and sinfonias have the opportunity for employing a countersubject along with the *first* entry of the subject, as opposed to *Well-Tempered-Clavier* fugues, which are unaccompanied from the beginning, and although this opportunity is sometimes taken advantage of, as, say, in Sinfonia Number Nine--which acquires a second countersubject along with its second entry--often it is not, and even Number Three, which also makes use of two countersubjects, introduces both for the first time along with the second entry. Number Fifteen has a countersubject which appears with every entry of the subject and answer, but there are only four complete entries throughout the piece. Number One has a countersubject which is not introduced until the opening system of entries has been completed, and the same is true of Number Seven. Number Five has a countersubject-like affair which is continuous and far more pervasive than the subject, itself, or its answer. Practices thus vary widely within this set of pieces.

Imitation plays a dominant role in all fifteen sinfonias, being found invariably at the beginning, where its applications are strictest, and also during interior portions, where its applications may be strict or free. Imitation involves restatement of a melodic line from one voice-part to another, and its employment virtually ensures at least some equality of voicing. In the *Sinfonias*, where this device usually affects all three voices, the most typical opening procedure has the second upper voice imitating the first at the dominant (the lower perfect fourth or upper perfect fifth) with what is known as an *answer*, after which the third entry (often coming in after a link) appears in the bass at the lower octave or double octave with the first entry; however, not all conform to this plan. Number Six, for example, utilizes a subject-answer-answer arrangement rather than subject-answer-subject, so its third entry appears at the lower octave with the *second* entry rather than the first. Numbers Two and Fifteen employ imitation at the *octave* instead of the fifth for the second entry (as in most of the *Two-Part Inventions*), a feature which makes the term *answer* less appropriate, since imitation at the octave functions more as a replica than response. In both of these sinfonias, there is no complete third entry, but rather an incomplete (*false*) entry (in the bass of Number Two and alto of Number Fifteen). Number Five is unique in that its bass does not present even so much as a fragment of the subject or answer within the opening system of entries (this system being termed an *exposition*) or anywhere within the piece.

Answers come in two different forms, *real* and *tonal*. Those which transpose the subject down a perfect fourth or up a perfect fifth exactly, into the dominant key or at the dominant position of the tonic key (the latter usually just in major) are termed *real* (see Numbers Four, Six, Seven, Nine, Ten, Eleven, and Thirteen). Those having an adjustment in the numerical size of one or more intervals so that *part* of the answer imitates at the lower fourth or upper fifth (as in the real answer) and another part imitates at the lower fifth or upper fourth (the reverse of what happens in the real answer) are termed *tonal*. The tonally adjusted portion (that which imitates at the lower fifth or upper fourth) responds to some specific characteristic of the subject which makes it desirable. Tonal answers are employed in five sinfonias: Numbers One and Eight (in response to subjects which begin on the fifth scale degree and end on the third), Three and Twelve (in response to modulating subjects), and Fourteen (in response to a subject having an initially filled-in tonic-to-dominant melodic movement). In minor-key sinfonias which employ an answer--real or tonal--the dominant *minor* key is used rather than the dominant major (which is not closely related) for the second entry.

After the answer has been stated as the second entry, a passage known as a *link* commonly appears (Numbers Four, Seven, Nine, Ten, Eleven, Thirteen, and Fourteen), usually effecting a change back to the tonic key. This link, sometimes in two voices and sometimes in three, normally makes use of derivative material, and in the *Sinfonias* (although not always in the *Well-Tempered-Clavier* fugues) it always equates in length with the subject; in two instances (Numbers Seven and Ten), it even features a restatement of the subject in transposition by at least one voice-part. A link does not usually appear when there is no modulatory need for it, as, for example, when the subject itself modulates to the dominant and the answer modulates back to the tonic (Numbers Three and Twelve), when the third entry is an answer rather than a subject (Number Six), or when the subject starts on the fifth scale degree, *and* the answer merely tonicizes the dominant *chord* rather than actually reaching the dominant *key* (Numbers One and Eight). A link is also avoided when the opening exposition has no complete third entry (Numbers Two and Fifteen) or no third entry at all (Number Five). The beginning exposition is, however, *usually* rounded out by a complete third entry and followed by an episode-- a passage (often modulatory) which separates isolated, or groups of subject (answer) entries from each other usually by developing fragments of previously stated material, especially the subject.

Generally, the same types of other devices found within a two-voice texture in the *Inventions* show up within a three-voice texture in the *Sinfonias*. Invertible counterpoint, in which one melodic line is situated above a second melodic line during one passage and <u>below</u> during another passage, is extremely important, as one might expect in view of the frequent employment of countersubjects, although not all passages exhibiting invertible counterpoint involve subject or answer statements, for the technique is also employed sometimes during episodes.

All the *Sinfonias* make use of invertible counter-point, some (such as Number Fourteen) in a rather skimpy manner, and others more abundantly. Within a three-voice texture, the opportunities for inversion are much more numerous than within a two-voice texture; however, much of the invertible counterpoint in these pieces is double (invertible two-part) counterpoint, involving on-ly two of the three melodic lines, even when a three-voice texture prevails. Triple (invertible three-part) counterpoint is found with varying degrees of incipien-cy, mostly in Numbers Three, Nine, Ten, and Thirteen, the first of these being the richest in this regard, since it manifests six out of the six possible arrange-ments for inversion, in every case with the subject and two countersubjects. Number Nine, although not as pro-lific in its arrangements of the subject along with two countersubjects, goes beyond the practice of Number Three by employing it during episodes, as well.

The *Sinfonias*, like the *Inventions* and the *Well-Tempered-Clavier* fugues, emphasize texture and contra-puntal lines, and most are remarkably continuous-sound-ing, having constant rhythmic flow which results from ingenious distribution of motion among the voice-parts. Only two (Numbers Six and Fifteen) have any cessation of motion prior to their final cadences, but all these pieces still tend to divide themselves into sections set off either by cadences which are harmonically con-clusive as well as rhythmically continuous, or by new treatment of material. The ultimate section-defining device, of course, is the cadence, and by far the most important type in the *Sinfonias* is the authentic ca-dence. The deceptive cadence and half cadence are also employed from time to time, but the plagal cadence is virtually non-existent.

A definite structural pattern can be observed in a majority of the *Sinfonias*--with or without any strong section-defining cadences--a pattern whereby a first sec-tion unfolds with an exposition followed by a modulato-ry episode, which (sometimes followed, in turn, by one or more additional entries of the generating idea) leads to the end of the section, and a second section which then begins in the new key exhibiting a different voic-ing arrangement with one or more statements of the sub-ject and/or answer. In the C-Minor Sinfonia (Number Two), in fact, most of the first section is restated in transposed invertible counterpoint during the second sec-tion (a condition which is also true of the C-Minor *In-*

*vention*). In the E-Minor Sinfonia (Number Seven) the
second section begins with a two-entry counterexposition, employing the same tonic and dominant keys employed during the exposition, but with different voicing.
Some sinfonias have just one complete, intact entry at
the beginning of section two; others, two entries; and
still others, three, but occasionally there is none at
all.

Most of the *Sinfonias* have return, or some sem-
blance of return--this being construed as the reappearance of the initial subject or motive in the tonic key
somewhere within the last part of the piece. Seldom,
however, is this return situated two-thirds of the way,
as one might expect, particularly in those pieces having three sections. The average seems to be something
more like five/sixths (as opposed to four/fifths in the
*Two-Part Inventions*), and the return does not necessari-
ly establish the beginning of a new section, but rather
may emerge as an ongoing part of the section already in
progress. Number Five's return is noteworthy in that it
brings back most of the opening section--an unusually
large amount--with the upper two voices exchanged in
invertible counterpoint. Number Eleven's return brings
back about half of the opening section with*out* invertible counterpoint, and this is additionally *pre*ceded by
a return of *later* material, from the second section.
Number Two has no return involving the opening subject,
but it does bring back a portion of the episode which
follows the initial entries of the piece (in a manner
somewhat reminiscent of what happens in the F-Major *Two-
Part Invention*), and Number Fifteen, which is much like
Number Two in its opening procedures, also avoids a complete restatement of the subject for a return, although
the subject's third measure comes back pretty much intact.

In terms of harmony, both triads and seventh chords
are used, or implied, in conjunction with both diatonic
and chromatic harmony. The principal altered chord is
the secondary dominant, which shows up in one form or
another, minimally or extensively in almost all of the
*Sinfonias*. Other, occasionally used types are the Neapolitan sixth chord and the borrowed chord, and the Picardy third is found in the final chord of all minor-key
sinfonias having a third at this point (Numbers Two,
Seven, Nine, and Thirteen). Modulation generally occurs only to keys which are closely related to the tonic key, and chromatic voice leading involving the cross
relation and chromatic half step may be found from time
to time. There are even occasional examples of the dou-

ble inflection (simultaneous cross relation). Nonharmonic tones of virtually every type are used copiously.

No discussion of the *Sinfonias* would be complete
without some mention of sequence, which is extremely
pervasive, like imitation and invertible counterpoint.
Sequence, which involves immediate, transposed (other
than at the octave), restatement in the same voice, is
exploited in a wide variety of ways, almost always being built out of derivative material, or such material
to which new material has been attached, in both modulatory and non-modulatory situations, strictly, freely,
and sometimes even built right into the subject and/or
countersubject (as in Numbers Three and Nine). It is
used considerably more than out-and-out repetition (which
is scarce), sometimes in conjunction with other devices
such as imitation, but often not, sometimes in just one
voice, other times in two voices simultaneously, and
still other times in all three. All the *Sinfonias* employ sequence during at least one passage, and most of
them employ it abundantly. Its importance as a spin-
ning-out device can not be emphasized strongly enough.

The contrapuntal style involving three voices--in
many ways the ideal number of voices, since it allows
for complete as well as incomplete triadic sonorities
with only half the possibilities for voice-leading prob-
lems having to do with pairs of voices (consecutive perfect fifths, octaves, and unisons) that exist in the
four-voice style--was preferred by Bach not just for the
*Sinfonias*, but additionally for the majority of fugues
in both volumes of the *Well-Tempered Clavier*. Consider-
ing the careful attention which Bach, himself, gave to
voice leading and the other "nitty-gritty" details of
composition, it seems almost certain that he insisted
upon the same type of attention on the part of his stu-
dents, but he avoided species counterpoint (which was
popularized slightly after the time the *Inventions* and
*Sinfonias* were printed, by J.J. Fux in *Gradus ad Parnas-
sum*, in 1725), and concentrated on teaching whole com-
positions rather than isolated fragments.

The *Sinfonias* reflect this approach, and like the
*Inventions*, they are not just exercises, but rather miniature masterpieces, deserving of intensive analytical
scrutiny by those who wish to achieve insight into Bach's
contrapuntal practices. Although they were originally
conceived for pedagogical purposes and are not programmed
frequently by concert artists today, they are as vital
and alive, now, on the three-hundredth anniversary of

his birth, as they were at the time they were composed.

November 1985                               Theodore O. Johnson

East Lansing, Michigan

# CHAPTER 1:   SINFONIA NUMBER ONE (C MAJOR)


The C-Major Sinfonia is probably best interpreted as a three-sectioned affair, with sections (measures 1-7, 7-15, and 15-21) not as well defined by cadences as by other musical conditions. The subject, or its answer, right-side-up or upside-down, is virtually ubiquitous throughout the piece (generating relentless sixteenth-note motion), but certain passages nevertheless take on the character of links or episodes. A countersubject does not appear during the opening exposition, although what one could call a countersubject--because of its subsequent intermittent re-employment (always above the subject or answer--never below) does show up later, during measure 5.

The subject begins on the fifth scale degree, in the soprano, just after the first beat of measure 1, exploiting sixteenth notes which are entirely conjunct until the beginning of the fourth beat. The alto's answer during measure 2 responds tonally in the conventional manner, its first note on the first scale degree-- still in C major--answering the fifth scale degree from the subject, with imitation at the fourth (lower fifth). Often with the answer responding to this type of subject, the tonal portion (that imitating at the fourth rather than the fifth) is minimal, and an early adjustment is made to render the bulk of the answer "real," but here--because of the scalewise nature of the generating idea--the tonal portion lasts throughout most of the entry, with the adjustment to imitation at the fifth (lower fourth) coming at the beginning of beat four. Because of this, it is not possible for the answer to do anything more than tonicize the dominant *chord* without any real modulation taking place. The overall effect is somewhat akin to that of a long, filled-in dominant scale degree resolving to the mediant within the subject, responded to with a long, filled-in tonic scale degree resolving to the leading tone within the answer.

1

No link is used between the second and third entries, the most traditional location, a circumstance relating to the fact that the subject--which is about to
enter at the lower octave in the bass--begins on the
fifth scale degree and can thus be harmonized with dominant (rather than, say, tonic six-four) harmony following the secondary dominant, providing contrast with the
soprano's opening subject. Alto-voice suspensions offer additional interest here.

Example 1-1.   Measures 1-4

An inverted tonal answer with an altered final note
begins at measure 4 in the bass and serves as a type of
non modulatory link between the opening system of three
entries and an additional (redundant) entry in the bass
starting in measure 5--a subject, down yet another octave. The soprano material of measure 5, although hard-
ly comprising a classic instance of the countersubject,
could perhaps be termed such because of its later appearances at measures 8-9 (up a fifth in the soprano),
19 (on the same pitch levels in the alto), and somewhat tentatively in both 14 and 15 (respectively transposed and untransposed in the soprano). Alto material
from measure 5 might be labelled countersubject two,
but it is even less pervasive (showing up again in the
alto, transposed, during measures 8-9, and in the soprano, at the upper octave, during 19). Suspensions are
abundant once again, and indeed, throughout the piece the
subject's appearance in the bass seems to call for sus-

pensions up above. An inversion of the tonal answer similar to the one at measure 4 comes about in 6, now in
the inner voice rather than the lowest, and again without any modulation, so with the imperfect authentic cadence of measures 6-7, the first section comes to an
end, still in the tonic key--a somewhat unusual feature.

Example 1-2.   Measures 4-7

        Section two begins episodically at measure 7, and
within its first one-and-one-half measures, upside-down
statements of the subject's first half are employed sequentially by the bass with three stages which rise by
degree.  Sequence is also suggested but not fully realized in the uppermost voice.  Change away from the
tonic key--which has pervaded the first six measures of
the piece--into the dominant key, occurs almost immediately.

        After this sequential episode has concluded, most
of the two-bar passage from measures 5-6 returns in G
major (from the middle of 8 to the middle of 10) with
transposition which is upward by perfect fifth in the
soprano and alto parts, and downward by perfect fourth
in the bass part, until octave displacement of the note
B during the last half of measure 9 changes the interval
of restatement to the upper fifth in the bass to match
that of the soprano and alto (Example 1-3).

        Following a deceptive harmonic progression in the

Example 1-3.   Measures 7-10

middle of measure 10, the soprano imitates the alto from
9 at the sixth, providing now a complete account of the
inverted tonal answer. Midway through this soprano account, the bass presents another upside-down version of
the answer, creating stretto at the seventh (lower ninth
plus an octave) with the soprano and setting up a modulation into D minor.

Example 1-4.   Measures 10-12

Beginning at measure 12 and continuing into 15, a
series of consecutive answer and subject entries are presented in imitation by the soprano, alto, and bass, respectively, the second entry being mostly located down
a second from the first, and the third, down an additional second (ninth). The first, beginning (measure 12)
on the second scale degree in D minor, is an answer which

has been modified through interval expansion in such a way that the natural and (ascending) melodic forms of the minor scale clash, creating an interesting and unusual double inflection (simultaneous cross relation) between Bb in the soprano and B-natural in the alto, the latter voice which--after momentarily resting--has taken the subject's first few notes in rhythmic augmentation. The accompaniment provided by the bass throughout this bar (12) is likewise based upon the subject's opening fragment in augmentation, but upside-down and extended by sequence (both treatment and material being reminiscent of a passage in the C-Major *Two*-Part Invention, at measures 19-20).

The second entry (at 13-14) is a subject beginning on D, the first scale degree of the key in which it commences, but more appropriately situated in the key in which it finishes (G minor), the leading-tone of which is approached chromatically in the soprano as the bass is engaging in a type of "mock" stretto with the alto by bringing in the subject's head in inversion. The third entry is also a subject, beginning on the fifth degree in F major, to which key the first chord of measure 14 pivots. A portion of countersubject one in the soprano accompanies this bass entry, while the alto supplies the second stage of a sequence based upon the preceding subject's tail motive.

Example 1-5. Measures 12-15

A sense of return is conveyed by the bass statement
of the subject on its original degrees within C major at
measure 15, although continuity is carried to an extreme,
because this statement comprises the second stage of a
sequence at the upper perfect fifth from measure 14, and
there is no cadential progression to assist the establishment of a new section. Furthermore, a fairly uncom-
mon suspension, the six/five-four, is applied to the
first beat, which has a pivot chord leading from F major to C major, eliciting an unstable effect. Like the
first stage of this sequence, this one is accompanied by
incomplete countersubject-one material in the soprano.

This bass subject starting in 15 is responded to by
a tonal answer in the alto during 16, but the answer
starts out imitating at the seventh rather than the
fourth, as originally, and it thus concludes by imitating at the octave rather than the fifth, as originally,
since, as a tonal answer, it encompasses an overall range
which is a second larger than that of the subject. In
other words, it starts on the fourth degree, and because
of its intervalic adjustment--here, into the fourth beat
of measure 16 in the alto--it concludes on the same
degrees as those for the subject, an octave higher.

During the final half of measure 16, an inverted
account of the tonal answer is begun in stretto by the
bass, which, once again, spawns employment of the suspension, in this instance a very unusual one, the six-
five, with its sixth--the alto's A in measure 17--ac-
quiring its dissonant characteristics from association
with the seventh of a secondary dominant chord of the
subdominant, the soprano's Bb in the same measure.

Example 1-6.   Measures 15-17

A brief episode takes over (as another alto-voice suspension--this one having an ornamented resolution--is unfolding) at the middle of measure 17, recalling the earlier episode found at the *beginning* of 7 and after, transposed up a perfect fourth both tonally (in G major before, and C major here) and melodically, at least in the bass, which has three stages of sequence on half of the inverted subject, the last half of 17 corresponding to the *first* half of 7, the first half of 18 corresponding to the *last* half of 7, etc. The upper voices exhibit less parallelism with the earlier passage, although they do exploit imitative fragments involving the subject's opening, both uninverted and inverted, as back in 7-8. The alto also has most of the subject's second and third beats, inverted, within measure 18.

Example 1-7.   Measures 17-19

By measure 19, however, as the bass continues paralleling the earlier passage, the upper voices join in, and compositely they bring back the one-measure passage starting in the middle of measure 8 (which originated at the beginning of 5) with the previous soprano line (countersubject one) being now located down a fifth in the alto, and the previous alto line (countersubject two), up a fourth in the soprano, creating invertible counterpoint at the octave.

During the penultimate measure (20) another statement of the inverted tonal answer begins in the top voice and migrates to the middle one, in a simulated

*durchbrochene-Arbeit* fashion.  It is accompanied by the
bass with a half-bar thought that is freely sequenced,
and the piece concludes as succinctly as it has unfold-
ed throughout.

Example 1-8.  Measures 19-21

## CHAPTER 2: SINFONIA NUMBER TWO (C MINOR)

Sinfonia Number Two is less typical than Number One, because instead of employing imitation at the fifth for its second entry, it makes use of imitation at the octave, in the manner of the conventional *two*-part invention. Moreover, it has no complete third entry by the bass, but rather a false (incomplete) entry. A similar opening plan may be found with the B-Minor Sinfonia (Number Fifteen), with different voicing.

The subject begins disjunctly, outlining the tonic triad during measure 1, and then continues conjunctly, forming a miniature palindrome as it ascends the harmonic minor scale on C to the sixth degree (Ab), drops a diminished seventh to the seventh degree (B-natural), then returns to the sixth degree only to descend most of the way back before concluding on Eb at the beginning of measure 3. The second measure of this subject is strikingly reminiscent of the generating idea of the D-Minor *Two*-Part Invention (Number Four). The bass material of measures 1-2, which produces all primary chords with the subject above it, does not comprise a true countersubject, for it has very limited and incomplete recurrence.

Imitation at the lower octave begins in the alto just as the subject itself is ending, and this imitation is strict throughout. The soprano, having finished with the subject, continues in counterpoint with the alto, as the bass drops out--creating a condition which is unique for this location among the *Sinfonias* of Bach. The soprano line of measures 3-4, like the bass line of 1-2, is not sufficiently recurrent to be logically construed as a countersubject (Example 2-1).

Measure 5 initiates a four-and-one-half bar episode based upon derivative material: the first six notes of the subject followed by a falling seventh, then a

9

Example 2-1.  Measures 1-5

rest, in the bass; the *rhythmic* pattern from the bass of
measure 2 in the soprano; and material from the second
measure of the subject in rhythmic diminution (with sixteenth notes rather than eighth notes) in the alto, which
avoids the falling diminished seventh from Ab to B-natural found in measure 2, supplanting it with a rising
major second from Ab to Bb. Each of these ideas is stated and then sequenced down one degree. The bass is giv-
en the better part of a third sequential stage during
the first half of measure 7, down one more degree, but
instead of rests in the last half of 7, the bass has an
intervalically adjusted version of the first half, as
the other voices' material becomes less derivative, although sequence is still employed by the alto, from the
middle of measure 7 to the middle of 8, strictly, and
almost so by the soprano from the middle of 8 to the
middle of 9, where the initial sixteenth-note group is
inverted (in relationship to previous appearances), and
its continuation is not. Modulations from C minor to Eb
major (measures 5-6) and Eb major to G minor (8-9) pro-
pel this passage forward, and the first section concludes with an imperfect authentic cadence in the dominant minor key within measure 9 (Example 2-2).

Most of the first section returns during section

Example 2-2.  Measures 5-9

two, with exchange of voice-parts through transposition
upward by fifth (or downward by fourth) from bass to alto and alto to soprano), and downward by eleventh, from
soprano to bass, so that what originally was the soprano
line and here is the bass line appears in invertible
counterpoint with one or both of the other lines.  This
second section begins with a bass statement of the full
subject (the bass's first such statement) in the dominant minor key, from the middle of measure 9 to the middle of 11, accompanied initially in the alto by most of
the material found in the bass during measure 1, at the
upper fifth, as the soprano supplies new material (A,
F♯, and G dotted quarter notes).  In the middle of measure 10, the alto temporarily abandons its transposition
of the bass material from before (measure 2) as the soprano rests (duplicating a portion of the alto rest from
measure 2), and shortly thereafter, the alto provides
doubling of the bass subject's closing portion at the
upper sixth.  The soprano (from the middle of 11 to the
middle of 13) imitates the bass from the beginning of

this second section at the upper octave, as the bass--
prior to becoming free (during the first half of 13)--
continues in the same way that the soprano continued during measures 3-4, after *it* had completed its first subject entry, and the alto (measure 12) brings in the soprano's three notes from 10, with octave displacement.

Example 2-3.   Measures 9-13

The ensuing episode rehashes most of the events of
the previous one in a similar way, even to the extent of
initially modulating the same distance (from G minor to
Bb major), in the same way, at the corresponding location (in the middle of measure 14).  The bass generally
remains faithful to the soprano from before, so that in
effect, the entire soprano line from measures 1-9 (section one) shows up as the bass line during 9-18 (a significant portion of section two) with certain modifications such as embellishment (at the beginning of 13),
octave displacement (starting with the trilled Bb in

15), and skeletonization (at the end of 16), besides, of course, transposition, which starts using imperfect as well as perfect intervals during 17 (in relationship to the soprano line during 8-9), where G minor returns, signaling an end to the paralleling process.

The upper two voices continue their respective lines from before with fewer modifications throughout most of this second episode, the alto (starting on the third beat of measure 13) bringing back the bass part (from the first beat of 5) at the upper perfect fifth, but with *un*dotted quarter notes replacing what previously were dotted quarters, and the soprano at the same location bringing back the alto, likewise up a perfect fifth until the very end of measure 15, where octave displacement changes the interval of transposition to the lower fourth, following which shorter values with rests supplant what previously were sustained notes.

Both upper voices become free early within measure 17--somewhat sooner than does the bass--the soprano, by restating its most recent two-note figure (F-D) at the upper sixth, with the original elongated second note, then sequencing it one degree higher, and the alto, by imitating the soprano at the lower fifth, in part. During the first half of measure 18, the alto imitates the bass from the first half of 17 at the upper double octave, and slightly before this imitation is over, the bass, in turn, presents most of this imitative idea upside-down, creating a loose stretto effect. The bass's last beat of 18, then, has the last portion of this idea right-side-up, as part of the authentic cadence which concludes the second section.

Example 2-4. Measures 13-19

The remainder of the piece is entirely episodic in nature, for there are no more complete statements of the subject. The third section begins in the dominant minor key (like the second section) with the first seven notes of the subject in the soprano, Db here creating a rising diminished, rather than perfect fifth and turning the minor tonic triad in G into a diminished supertonic triad in F minor. After having been restruck, this Db is sustained, as soprano material from the first part of measure 5 is brought in by the alto, with interval contraction, and soprano material from the *last* part of 8 is brought in by the bass, giving rise to a double inflection (between D-natural and Db).

During the first half of measure 20, the bass freely sequences itself from the last half of 19, as the soprano presents another version of the subject's head, also modified by means of interval contraction, but in a different way (creating, among other things, a melodic augmented fourth). Free imitation of the bass by the alto during the last half of 20, where a modulation into Eb major takes place, results in another transposed statement of the sixteenth-note soprano configuration from the last half of 8. New accounts of the subject's head motive occur during the following measures (21 and 22) in the alto voice in alternation or conjunction with sixteenth-note groupings which resemble the sixteenth-note motive from measure 8, now in the soprano again, as the bass first rests, then becomes slightly sequential with a conjunct idea founded on the eighth-note/quarter-note rhythm from measure 2.

Example 2-5.  Measures 19-22

In the middle of measure 22, a sequence evolves in all three voices almost simultaneously, the bass employing the sixteenth-note motive as it was originally found during 5, but rounded off in a more sustained fashion (without rests), and the soprano and alto, elongated notes followed, respectively, by a modified account of the subject's first four notes, and material which is mostly free. There are three one-bar stages in the bass, lasting until the middle of 25, but only about two-and-one-half in the upper two voices, the last incomplete stage of which in the soprano is approached by an augmented fifth (from B-natural to Eb in 24).

During the first half of 25, as the bass is completing the third stage of its sequence, these upper voices break off, the middle voice in order to rest mo-

mentarily, and the upper voice to present a version of
the sixteenth-note motive from measures 8-9, and else-
where--a version which is then imitated by the alto down
a ninth during the last half of 25, and by the bass down
an additional ninth (starting on F) during the first
half of 26. A suggestion of the subject's opening is
provided by the alto in syncopated form with a melodic
augmented fourth (similar to one found in the soprano
earlier, in measure 20) the upper note of which (B) resolves as an ornamented retardation in conjunction with
the resolution of a suspension in the soprano during
measure 26. Another suspension, now in the alto, initiates a retrograde (or inversion) of the first six notes
of the subject's second measure, during the first half
of 27, which then becomes free, leading into the strong-
est cadence of the piece, so far--a perfect authentic
cadence, at measures 27-28.

Example 2-6.   Measures 22-28

This cadence marks the recurrence of a passage from the first episode (at measures 5 and after) in altered form, providing the only sense of return found in the sinfonia. In the alto, measure 28 corresponds exactly to measure 5, but in the outer voices modifications have been made, the bass being down an octave during its first half and sequential (at the upper fourth) during its second half. The soprano's falling fifth into beat three as opposed to its falling seventh before, is also note-worthy. Measure 29, furthermore, is obviously based upon 6, but with changes which occur mostly because the bass drops out, leaving the alto to assume most of its role, as the soprano does service for both the soprano and alto lines from before, the earlier alto line, from the last half of 6 being situated up an octave in the soprano here, as the alto, itself, provides something *not* found during the last half of 6, another statement of the subject's first six notes, focusing about the mediant triad, which has been tonicized by its own secondary dominant chord during the first half of 29.

Measure 30 brings back the events of measure 7 in all three voice-parts transposed mostly down a third, and during the first half of 31, the paralleling procedure continues in the bass, which has the bass line from measure 8, likewise down a third, doubled momentarily by the soprano at the upper tenth on beat two. A falling augmented fifth from B-natural to Eb in the bass (like the earlier one in the soprano during 24) sets

up a highly ornamented suspension in the alto, which--as
it ascends and descends fragments of the melodic-minor
scale--provides at least a suggestion of the original
sixteenth-note motive from measure 5.  Additional such
suggestions by the soprano and bass in contrary motion
on the first beat of 32 lead into a cadential six-four
chord followed by the final cadence, which exploits a
Picardy third.

Example 2-7.   Measures 28-32

# CHAPTER 3:  SINFONIA NUMBER THREE (D MAJOR)

Triple (invertible three-part) counterpoint resulting from the use of two countersubjects along with statements of the subject and answer, plays a dominant role
in this sinfonia, exhibiting all six possible arrange-
ments of the three melodic lines in relationship to each
other--a real *tour de force* with a subject of the length
employed here within the framework of just twenty-five
measures, especially since neither of the two countersubjects appears during measures 1-3 in the bass along
with the opening soprano entry.

The subject, which begins sequentially with three
two-beat stages--the first tonicizing and resolving to
the subdominant--and then continues with two one-beat
stages (during the last half of measure 2 as it leads
into 3), is best construed as concluding on the third
(rather than the first) beat of measure 3, since the
afterthought-like appendage which modulates to the dominant key during the first part of this measure shows
up along with five of the seven subject or answer entries of the sinfonia, its omission from the final two
entries (measures 21-25)--the second of which also o-
mits the few notes which precede it--serving to pre-
vent a modulation away from the tonic key so close to
the end of the piece.

Example 3-1.  Measures 1-3

19

The alto's response to this subject extends from the middle of measure 3 to the beginning of 6, imitating in the dominant key, at the fifth (lower fourth) until the last three notes of measure 5, where it switches to imitation at the fourth (lower fifth) for its closing portion, which therefore accommodates a modulation from A major back to D major (tonal movement upward by fourth) in response to the subject's modulation from D major to A major (tonal movement upward by fifth).

Beneath this tonal answer, the bass starts out by presenting a series of sixteenth notes, which relate, in two four-note groups, to the subject's final six-teenth-note configuration on the second beat of measure 3 in the soprano (which has a transposed retrograde of the first beat) first right-side-up, and then upside-down. Two-beat sequential groupings in the bass (start-ing with its second sixteenth-note), which pretty much jibe with the initial two-beat sequential groupings of the alto's answer, tonicize and resolve to the super-tonic in A major before continuing and then giving way to a transposed statement of the eighth-note material from the last half of measure 2, during the first half of 5, as the answer changes to *its* one-beat sequential groupings. Less systematically organized sixteenths in the last half of measure 5 provide counterpoint to the answer's conclusion.

The initial sixteenth-note portion of this bass line can be termed countersubject one, commencing as it does just prior to the much less active soprano line--countersubject two--which descends conjunctly from E to C# in a fairly slow syncopated manner, then momentarily doubles the alto's answer at the upper third in six-teenth notes before becoming less active once again.

Example 3-2.  Measures 3-6

Because of the nature of this subject and its answer, there is no modulatory need for a link between
the second and third entries of the opening exposition,
and, in fact, none is employed, for the bass launches
its entry of the subject at the beginning of measure 6--
starting a perfect twelfth down from the alto entry of
measures 3-6 (a double octave down from the initial soprano entry)--while countersubject one, having moved up
an eleventh from the bass to the soprano, is now situated in invertible counterpoint with the subject, as
well as countersubject two, which, in turn, has moved
down a perfect fifth from the soprano to the alto.  If
the voice-parts were to be labelled ABC from top to bottom for the passage starting during the last half of
measure 3, they could be labelled CAB for the passage
starting at 6.  After dropping countersubject two, the
alto expands upon the process begun by countersubject
two before by doubling most of what is left of the subject at the upper tenth (measures 7-8).  Shortly after
having finished with countersubject one--which works to
tonicize the supertonic (as with the preceding answer,
rather than the subdominant, which was tonicized during
the original subject statement)--the soprano continues
accompanying the bass subject during the first half of
8 by presenting a new thought.

This new thought is then imitated by the bass at the
lower eleventh, as the soprano, in turn, imitates the
subject's tail motive at the upper twelfth, producing
invertible counterpoint at the triple octave (during the
last half of 8 in relationship to the first half).  The
one-bar soprano pattern (starting with the second note
of measure 8) is then sequenced up a second, continuing
its imitation of the bass in a canonical manner, but
only about half of the corresponding bass line is so
treated.  Harmonic movement from tonic to dominant in D
major during the first stage, and from supertonic to
submediant during the second, leads to a Phrygian-like
cadence in B minor (measures 9-10), softened by a sus-

pension in the middle voice.

Example 3-3.   Measures 6-10

The entry which appears in the soprano during measures 10-12 is a tonal answer, rather than a subject,
despite the fact that it begins--and remains most of the
way--in B minor, then modulates to F♯ minor, which lies
up a fifth, rather than E minor, which lies up a fourth
and would retain the original relationship of the answer.  The soprano's E♯ at the beginning of the third
beat of measure 12 functions to some extent as the answer's final note displaced downward by an octave (creating a diminished seventh rather than an augmented second melodic interval), and it confirms the key of F♯
minor, other ingredients of which precede it in the middle voice.  This middle voice has carried most but not
all of countersubject one starting near the beginning
of measure 10 in conjunction with the bass, which has
even less of countersubject two. Letter symbology based
upon the original association of the two countersubjects
with the answer at measure 3 and after can be defined
here as BCA from top to bottom.

Both lower voices acquire a configuration involving
the last four notes of the subject during measure 11, a
configuration which--both right-side-up and upside-down--
becomes the principal material of the *upper* two voices
during the initial portion of a long episode which starts
in the middle of measure 12.  Here, the soprano and al-

to--each having descending sequential stages within it-
self--operate in contrary motion until the beginning
of 14, where the soprano reverses direction. The bass
part is less rigid, although it does, during the interior beats of measure 13, display both the alto's
downward and the soprano's upward version conjoined
in such a way as to resurrect a half-measure segment
of countersubject one (originally found in the bass
from the last beat of measure 3 through the first beat
of 4). At the beginning of measure 14, its revival of
the eighth-note melodic scheme, in transposition, from
the last half of measure 2 paves the way for a perfect
authentic cadence in F♯ minor, the mediant-minor key.

Example 3-4.  Measures 10-14

The bass line which gets under way following the
cadence in measure 14 is a six-beat affair which is
stated and then sequenced virtually in its entirety
starting within the second beat of measure 16. The
first seven notes of each sequential stage are the *last*

seven notes of the subject, transposed, and after a
brief intervention, the last five notes of each stage
are the *first* five notes of the subject, both transposed and otherwise modified. A modulation into E minor accompanies the first stage, and one into D major,
the second stage, which is situated melodically as well
as tonally down one degree.

The upper voices behave compositely in a somewhat
similar manner, with the subject's head motive on its
original pitches (from measure 1) in the soprano in E
minor (rather than D major as back at the beginning),
followed by imitation at the lower octave in the alto a
half measure later, followed, in turn, by most of the
subject's seventh and eighth beats (originally from the
last half of measure 2) back in the soprano again and
on the appropriate scale degrees for E minor--all in
conjunction with the bass's first sequential stage. A-
long with the second stage, these same events transpire
down one degree, but with the two upper voices exchanged
in invertible counterpoint at the double octave, the
alto now leading off a ninth down from where the soprano
led off six beats earlier, and the soprano imitating
the alto at the upper octave (a seventh up from where
the alto appears six beats earlier).

The last half of measure 17 leading into 18 brings
back slightly more of the subject's closing portion than
has been found recently in the bass, now in the soprano
up a third from where it might be expected to lie in order to unite with its predecessor in the alto, as the
key switches to G major, and the harmonic rhythm becomes
more deliberate, with dominant harmony which prevails
throughout measure 18 before resolving to the tonic chord
of an imperfect authentic cadence in measure 19. Varied
head-motive material from the subject in the alto and
tail-motive material (involving mostly transposed statements of the sixteenth-note idea from the second beat of
measure 3) in the soprano provide the principal derivative melodic ideas of measure 18.

Example 3-5.   Measures 14-19

Measure 19 inaugurates a new series of entries, the first being a subject in the bass starting in G major, the subdominant major key, which allows for an ending in D major, the tonic key, so that the subsequent answer can effect a sense of return (a condition which is also present in Sinfonia Five). Countersubject one, emerging one sixteenth note later than customarily in relationship to the starting point of the subject, begins in the soprano and then migrates to the alto within the second beat. Countersubject two in the soprano, therefore, is also slightly deferred (by half a beat) until after the initial portion of countersubject one has been relayed to the alto. This arrangement of voices, which can be symbolized from top to bottom as ACB, places the subject and countersubject one in invertible counterpoint with each other (in relationship to the events of measure 3 and after), but neither of the other two voice-pairs. The alto, having completed countersubject one, becomes silent during the last half of 20 and the first half of 21, as the soprano reintroduces a transposed portion of the eighth-note bass line from the final half of measure 2, with octave displacement, then moves into sixteenth notes which resemble those opening countersubject one.

During the last half of measure 21, then, as an answer to the preceding entry, the alto contributes a statement which re-establishes the pitch classes of the opening subject of the sinfonia--up until the middle of 23, anyway, at which point it breaks off without including the material originally found in the soprano during the first half of 3, thus supplying the first incomplete rendering of the subject or answer. Countersubject one, getting under way one note late (as back in measure 19) appears in the soprano, and countersubject two in the bass, so during this passage each line is inverted with each other line from the original generating passage at the last half of measure 3 and after (each pair exhibiting a different interval of inversion in terms of the

octave, double octave, and triple octave). The appropriate symbolization of melodic lines from top to bottom here is CBA.

The final entry of the piece--which is even less
complete than the one before it--appears in the soprano,
interrupting the alto entry from before with upper-octave imitation, accompanied by countersubject two just
beneath it, and countersubject one on the bottom, so
that the letter symbology BAC from top to bottom can be
employed (completing the six possible manifestations of
triple counterpoint). Countersubject one in the bass
is followed by the eighth-note material from the last
half of measure 2, again (as in measure 20) making use
of octave displacement, during the first half of 25.
This incomplete version of the subject occurs at exactly the same pitch levels as those used for the very o-
pening statement, and its avoidance of the modulatory
ending portion allows the sinfonia to conclude almost
immediately, with a perfect authentic cadence in D major.

Example 3-6.   Measures 19-25

# CHAPTER 4:  SINFONIA NUMBER FOUR (D MINOR)

The short soprano subject which generates the D-Minor Sinfonia is based on a half-bar motive plus its restatement, mostly at the upper second, during measure 1, where an accompanying countersubject unfolds in corresponding half-bar sequential stages, the second stage at the upper fifth with the first. The alto, which rests during the first measure, presents a real answer in the dominant minor key by imitating the soprano at the fifth (lower fourth) beginning along with the resolution of a suspension (one of many suspensions found throughout this sinfonia) in the soprano early in measure 2, and ending with the resolution of its own suspension at the corresponding location in measure 3. During the first part of measure 2, the bass additionally imitates the soprano in stretto at the lower perfect eleventh and a one-beat time interval, becoming free on beat four, just after the soprano, by temporarily doubling the alto at the sixth, provides a fragment of the generating idea.

Measure 3 is mostly given over to a link in which the alto has a transposed altered version of the subject's opening (characterized by melodic inversion into the second beat) in a descending sequential fashion, and the soprano imitates the alto at the second, somewhat canonically, with a one-beat time interval (like that used between the bass and soprano in measure 2), while the alto simultaneously imitates the soprano at the lower third.  During this link, which modulates from A minor back to D minor, the bass drops out, a feature which calls attention to its re-entry with the subject in measure 4, two octaves down from the soprano's opening entry in measure 1.  This bass subject is accompanied by mostly underivative material in the soprano and alto, although the soprano's fourth beat does relate back to the subject's very opening (Example 4-1).

Example 4-1.   Measures 1-5

Measure 5 gets a passage under way with sequence in all three voices, the soprano imitating the alto, as in measure 3 but at the sixth rather than the second, with a four-note (half-bar) version of the subject's head portion characterized by interval expansion into its second beat. The accompanying bass line relates back to the soprano line from the first half of measure 2 (also with interval expansion) causing the bass from the beginning of its entry in measure 4 to be intact with the original soprano line slightly longer than was the alto (starting in measure 2). A key change into F major takes place within measure 5.

The principal thematic event of measure *6* is the bass's account of the subject, intervalically enlarged in such a way that the second and third beats give rise to the first stage of a sequence, the second stage of which comes at the upper perfect fourth during the subsequent two beats, after which the bass reverts to a succession of eighth notes that provide the better part of an evened-out third stage, up yet another perfect fourth, as the passage briefly tonicizes and resolves to the subdominant triad in F major.

The upper voices meanwhile (measure 6) temporarily continue their use of sustained notes alternating with sixteenth notes on a beat-by-beat basis. During the first half of 7, the alto presents the subject's second beat (with interval contraction) followed by its third, after which the soprano features several transpositions of the subject's first three notes, prefixed and suffixed in various ways as they lead into the end of the first section in the middle of measure 8, accompanied more or less freely by the other two voices.

Example 4-2.   Measures 5-8

The new section's opening is characterized by an appearance of the subject in the alto, intermittently doubled at the upper sixth by the soprano and accompanied by the bass with the countersubject from measure 1 (all within the key of F major) followed by a soprano statement of the subject in imitation at the upper octave, doubled intermittently by the alto at the lower third in such a way as to create invertible counterpoint with the immediately preceding statement, and accompanied by the bass with the countersubject up an octave. The subject's endings are treated in the same nonharmonic fashion as before, and the intermittent doubling procedure produces double suspensions (in the middle of measure 9 and measure 10).

During the last half of measure 10, the bass simulates the beginning of an answer, but its intervals into and within the eighth-note portion are widened, and the resulting half-bar unit becomes the point-of-departure for a three-stage sequence, as the passage moves through D minor in measure 11, on its way to A minor. While this bass sequence is unfolding, the upper voices engage in their previous practice of alternating sustained notes with sixteenths in opposition to each other, the sixteenths sometimes suggesting the first beat of the subject. In measure 12, the soprano becomes sequential with an intervalically adjusted account of the subject's first half, while the bass is almost sequential with an even more distorted version, and the alto (starting with its second beat) initiates a descent by chromatic and diatonic half step which lasts almost all the way to the cadence in the middle of measure 13.

Harmonically, the passage just before and during this descent is--along with the passage based upon it at the conclusion of the piece--one of the most colorful passages in Bach's *Sinfonias*. The first-inversion Bb-major triad at the end of measure 11 serves to pivot as a submediant triad in D minor, into a Neapolitan sixth chord in A minor, setting off, with its diminished-third melodic resolution in the alto, a harmonic rhythm which quickens considerably as a result of chord changes every half-beat. Within measure 12, the sixteenth-note groupings' interior portions, in both the soprano and bass, involve *unaccented* passing tones followed by *accented* neighboring tones, and the alto's descending chromaticism is accommodated within the framework of fairly standard chord progressions: the submediant (six-four) triad accommodating F♯; the supertonic triad, F-natural; the dominant (six-five) chord followed by the tonic, E; the leading-tone triad of the dominant, D♯; and the leading-tone triad, D-natural.

Measure 13's sixteenth-note groupings have nonharmonic-tone arrangements which are different from those used in 12, the first note of each four-note group now functioning as a suspension, and the second, as its resolution, although the third still functions as an accented neighboring tone. One more secondary dominant chord is used, on the second half of beat one (a leading tone seventh chord of the dominant), accommodating C-natural from the alto's descending melodic line as its seventh, just after C♯, the third of a major tonic triad (which briefly suggests a non closely related key). The ensuing dominant triad is the penultimate chord of a perfect authentic cadence concluding another section of the sinfonia (Example 4-3).

A third section begins in the middle of measure 13, and for quite some time it employs statements of the subject and answer, one right after another, the sub-

Example 4-3.  Measures 8-13

jects being strict within the prevailing tonal framework at any given time, and the answers, somewhat free,
initially resembling *tonal* answers in the way they re-
spond.  The first entry is a subject in the soprano, in
A minor, accompanied by the countersubject in the bass,
while the alto rests prior to providing imitation which
commences at the lower fourth in the middle of measure
14, switches for one note (A on the first half of beat
four) to imitation at the lower fifth, and then reverts
to the original interval of imitation, somewhat in the
manner of a tonal answer; however, despite the appearance of D♯ as a lower neighboring tone, the key utilized
here is *not* E minor (the key having a dominant relationship to A minor from before, although one not closely
related to the key of the sinfonia) but rather G minor,
which is achieved through a chromatic modulation having

an abrupt cross relation, that occurs from the third to the fourth beat of measure 14 (between E-natural and and Eb). This answer arrives on the appropriate scale degrees for G minor very late, on the second beat of measure 15. It is initially doubled by the soprano a sixth higher, then *imitated* by the bass a sixth lower, after which its accompanying voices become freer.

From the middle of measure 15 to the middle of 16, the bass has a strict subject statement in the subdominant minor key (G), accompanied as it starts out, by embellished material from the subject's first beat in the alto, and this bass statement is then responded to by the soprano (at 16-17) in much the same fashion that the soprano statement at 13-14 was responded to by the alto (at 14-15), with a modulation downward by another degree to F major, to match. A fragment of the countersubject in the bass accompanies its last half.

As part of this extended series of consecutive entries, the alto presents a final entry (from the middle of 17 to the middle of 18), starting in F major on the appropriate scale degrees and ending in D minor, also on the appropriate degrees, after interval expansion has taken place during the first half of 18, in conjunction with an inverted half-bar fragment of the countersubject in the bass.

This modified tail portion of the subject found in the alto during the first half of 18 is sequenced at the lower second during the second half, after which the alto continues with a two-beat, sixteenth-note unit that is imitated by the soprano at the upper fourth, as the bass once again brings in half of the countersubject. Harmonic as well as nonharmonic usages--particularly those involving the suspension once again--render this passage very expressive, as the harmonic rhythm quickens to reflect chord changes on the half beat, as in certain previous passages, the Neapolitan sixth chord on the first half of beat two in measure 19 standing out just before the voice-parts start to converge into close spacing, which becomes clustered at the beginning of measure 20, where an ornamented suspension with a change-of-bass occurs (Example 4-4).

The bass at measures 20-21 returns the original subject intact in the tonic key but with a concluding F♯ which, along with the alto's C-natural, tonicizes the subdominant triad. Chromatically rising eighth notes in the soprano during the last half of 20 continue the colorful harmonic effects from before during this bass

Example 4-4. Measures 13-20

statement of the subject, which has a deferred answer
at the subdominant level in the alto beginning in the
middle of measure 21--an answer which is strict until
just before its ending, where interval contraction causes it to conclude on the conventional scale degrees for
D minor.

Measures 22-23 recall 12-13, with the upper two
voices situated in invertible counterpoint at the octave with themselves from before, within the tonic key,
of course, rather than the dominant.  The soprano line
from 12-13 shows up here at 22-23 in the alto down a
perfect fifth, while the alto line--starting on beat
two--comes back here in the soprano up a perfect fourth,
encompassing, along with the material from just before,
eleven/twelfths of the descending chromatic scale on D.
On beat *three* of measure 22, then, the bass--just after
having defined another Neapolitan chord, now in root
position--brings back the bass line from the earlier
passage down a perfect fifth.  So this third section,
which concludes the piece, ends almost exactly like the
second section, in transposition from the dominant key
to the tonic.

Example 4-5.   Measures 20-23

## CHAPTER 5:  SINFONIA NUMBER FIVE (Eb MAJOR)

Sinfonia Number Five, like Numbers Two and Fifteen, does not treat all three voice-parts equally at the beginning, and, in fact, the bass, having not been given either the opening soprano motive or its answer, plays a role which is accompanimental throughout the piece. Its three-beat rhythmic pattern consisting of three sixteenth notes followed by two quarter notes, the first two beats of which almost consistently outline a root-position triad or (occasionally) a seventh chord, is broken at only two interior locations (measures 11-12 and 27-28), which are structurally significant in terms of being about equidistant, respectively, from the beginning and ending of the sinfonia, the first closing out the first section, and the second closing the section which sets up the return. The two interior points (other than 12 and 28) where the bass's first two beats do *not* outline a root-position triad or seventh chord, measures 16 and 24, both set up perfect authentic cadences that close smaller divisions.

The highly ornamented generating motive has its beginning deferred until near the end of measure 1 (providing the only instance of such delay in the *Sinfonias*). It is presented by the soprano, starting on the fifth scale degree, a condition often calling for tonal imitation which has the answer starting on the first degree, but it ends on the leading tone--a less traditional ending point--and the alto responds by starting on F instead of Eb, although its imitation does not lie completely at the lower *perfect* fourth, as in a typical *real* answer. Therefore, the answer, which is mostly doubled at the upper third by the soprano, ends on Ab, the root of a *sub*dominant chord, which has just been tonicized by its own secondary dominant, still in Eb major, whereas the opening motive's final note (D) in the soprano (measure 2) functions as the *third* of a *dominant* chord.

The bass outlines tonic harmony during the first two beats of measure 1, and dominant and subdominant harmony, respectively, during the corresponding parts of measures 2 and 3, dropping a third on the third beat of each of these bars to establish a pattern of harmonic rhythm which persists even after the size of the falling bass interval changes. The characteristic rhythm of the opening motive and its answer is employed about as relentlessly by the upper voices (sometimes ornamented) as is that of the bass, faltering only during those measures that precede interior cadence points, measures 11-12, 16, 24, and 27-28, the first and last of which feature hemiola.

The soprano material used to accompany the alto's answer during measures 2-3 is united with the previous opening soprano motive to form a two-measure unit (measures 1-3) which is then sequenced up one degree (3-5), and since the alto also employs this material--which thus functions somewhat like a countermotive--along with the beginning of the soprano's second sequential stage (measures 3-4), creating invertible counterpoint at the octave as it does so, and then goes ahead to *start* a second sequential stage of its own, a brief canon results between the upper two voices during the first five measures, with the alto consistently imitating the soprano at the lower fourth in such a way that four consecutive statements of the motive or its answer appear in an alternating fashion, moving downward by fourth or upward by fifth.

Example 5-1.   Measures 1-5

During the opening part of the episodic passage which follows, the bass--which has been exhibiting sequential behavior too--continues with essentially the same idea now with a falling *fifth* into the third beat of the measure, creating consecutive root movement by descending fifth which lasts for better than two measures, still with the same lopsided harmonic rhythm, as the soprano retains only the opening perfect fourth and the rhythmic scheme of the original motive, providing new sequential treatment which jibes with that found in the bass (measures 5-6). The alto, starting with the resolution of a nine-eight suspension in measure 7, sets out to imitate the soprano at the lower fifth (with a two-bar time interval of imitation), but becomes free by providing a version of the motive which is closer to the original version, at measures 8-9, in lieu of an exact second stage to the sequence.

Example 5-2.  Measures 5-9

As the bass (measure 9) revives its original thought from measure 1 down an octave, another variant of the opening motive is brought in by the alto and then taken up by the soprano in imitation a second higher, as the bass line is being sequenced at the upper *fourth*. The relative minor key starts to assert itself during this passage, and about the first true rhythmic variety of the sinfonia, other than that produced by ornamentation, in the upper voices compositely on the one hand

and the bass on the other, transpires during measures
11-12, where three two-beat units on top convey the effect of hemiola, enhancing the perfect authentic cadence
(measures 12-13) which concludes the first section of
this work. Nonharmonic activity in the form of a double suspension during the first part of measure 12,
followed, after an intervening cadential six-four chord,
by an anticipation at the very end of 12, as well as
the relief offered by changes in the bass's rhythmic
scheme (in addition to the tonal change and the treble's hemiola), call much attention to this structural
point of the piece.

Example 5-3.   Measures 9-13

The four-bar passage at measures 13-17 is also concluded by a perfect authentic cadence with an anticipation preceded by a cadential six-four chord, as well as
a break in the treble rhythmic pattern. The cadence
occurs in the dominant major key, and most of the passage, in fact, lies within this key (Bb major). The
alto's motive statement in 13-14 begins on the original
scale degrees as applied to C minor, but interval expansion (like that found in the alto part during measures 8-9) into its penultimate note (the grace note Bb)
causes it to end on the appropriate degree in Bb major
(the leading-tone, A-natural), and it is then imitated
by the soprano at the upper perfect fourth during measures 14-15, with the same type of interval expansion,
but all within the same key, Bb major. The bass line
here reflects the key change downward by second from C
minor to Bb major through the use of sequential movement

upward by fourth--rather than by fifth--to match the
downward-by-fourth sequential movement it manifests during the first two measures of the sinfonia, where no
true modulation takes place. The bass even begins a
third sequential stage up yet another fourth in measure
15, but its reaffirmation of the original falling third
at the end of the bar is at variance with the preceding
stages' falling sixths. The countersubject-like thought
from the soprano at the end of measure 2 and beginning
of 3 (and alto, a measure later) doubled in thirds between the two upper voices at the end of 15 and beginning of 16 sets the stage for melodic and rhythmic free-
doms exhibited by the material which leads into and forms
the cadence.

Example 5-4.  Measures 13-17

The new section at measure 17 and after begins in
a somewhat unstable manner, passing briefly through Eb
major and Ab major before settling into F minor, which
lasts slightly beyond the cadence at 24-25. A new variant of the original motive distinguished by descending
conjunct motion into its second note--a feature which
causes it to conclude on the third degree after having
begun on the fifth--is presented by the soprano during measures 17-18. This variant is imitated at the
lower perfect fifth by the alto (measures 18-19), and
then freely restated in transposition still in the alto,

starting at the lower second and continuing at the lower third, as the passage moves tonally down a third,
into F minor.   The bass line accompanying the treble e-
vents of measures 17-18-19 takes its cue from the bass
line of 13-14-15, at the upper seventh with the earlier
passage for two measures, then at the lower second for
most of an additional one.

Example 5-5.   Measures 17-20

The bass line of measures 20-21-22, however, has
been taken from measures 1-2-3, first at the lower seventh and then at the upper second, which might suggest
a complete rehash of the events from the first three
measures, in F minor, but only the first entry of the
original motive is put forward, by the soprano at 20-
21.   Instead of an intact answer in the alto then, a
variant similar to that used at measures 9-10--but without octave displacement--shows up in the soprano during
21-22 and then again with transpositions and additional
embellishment during 22-23. The alto part is freer still,
although it does support the soprano part during 21,
mostly doubled in thirds, and again at the end of 23,
as well as all the way through 24 and on into 25, in
sixths, suggesting (along with the soprano) a modified
version of the original motive (starting on the last
sixteenth of 23), as it does.   The bass retains its ris-
ing-arpeggiated-triad/falling-third format until the last
beat of measure 23, then becomes free prior to the F-
minor cadence, which is strengthened by another caden-

tial six-four chord and a double anticipation.

Example 5-6.   Measures 20-25

The four-measure passage at 25-29 corresponds in size and reverse structural location to the passage at 13-17, then, for the earlier one follows the end of the opening section, and this one precedes the beginning of the final section, most of which encompasses a return. The bass scheme from measure 13 through most of 15 comes back here at the upper fourth, having begun in C minor there and F minor here; however, this latter passage moves into Ab major (as opposed to Bb major before), thus setting off a different relationship of keys, and it also exploits one final variant of the original motive, first in the alto at 25-26, as the soprano is resting, and then imitatively in the soprano at the upper fourth, one measure later. A hemiola pattern similar to the one used at 11-12 then shows up--measure 28 being es-

sentially a transposition of 12 at the lower third (from
C minor there to Ab major here), so the same attention-
capturing features found at the conclusion of section
one are found here at the conclusion of this passage
which precedes the final section.

Example 5-7.   Measures 25-29

Following the Ab-major cadence at 28-29, the original opening motive, without any changes other than those
having to do with transposition, is asserted by the soprano, accompanied by the original bass line on the appropriate scale degrees for, and within the key of Ab
major.  The alto, having rested, resumes then with an
answer at the lower fourth in Eb major, which is, of
course, at the same time the dominant of Ab--key of the
previous motive entry--and tonic key of the movement, so
that the principal effect of return here, within the
tonic key, results from an entry functioning as an *answer* rather than the motive or subject itself, a time-
honored procedure in other contrapuntal works by Bach
(for example, the D-Major Sinfonia).

This return then goes ahead to corroborate most of
the opening section of the sinfonia, but with the upper
two voices exchanged in invertible counterpoint at the
octave.  The alto, for example, starting in the last
half of measure 30 and continuing into the final measure of the piece, duplicates the soprano starting in
the last half of measure 1 and continuing into measure

9, strictly (except for details concerning ornamentation), at the lower octave, and the soprano, starting
one measure later (in the last half of 31) duplicates
the alto (from the last half of 2) at the unison, *almost*
strictly (being slightly free at the end of 33 and beginning of 34, and also varying in certain details of
ornamentation). The bass part is like that from the beginning too except for its lower-octave transposition
during measure 30 in relationship to measure 1. Without
any of the previously observed strengthening devices
such as hemiola or the cadential six-four chord, and
with an escape tone at the end of 37 supplanting what
at all previous cadence points has been an anticipation,
the final cadence is weaker than any of its interior
predecessors, bringing the sinfonia to an end rather
serenely.

Example 5-8.   Measures 29-38

# CHAPTER 6: SINFONIA NUMBER SIX (E MAJOR)

The E-Major Sinfonia, in compound meter like Sinfonias Two and Fifteen (and Two-Part Inventions Ten and Twelve), is singular among this group of fifteen pieces in that its opening exposition features *two* answers in response to the opening idea rather than one answer followed by the original idea at another octave level--the usual procedure. This idea, which is more of a motive than a true subject, unfolds in the alto with conjunct rising eighth notes lasting from the beginning of beat one until the beginning of beat three within measure 1, where change of direction sets off a type of changing-tone configuration, the first note of which (C#) is non-harmonic to the third beat's dominant harmony, and the second note of which (A) provides a seventh that resolves into the final note of the generating motive on beat one of the following measure. Throughout most of the piece, similar treatment prevails with entries of this motive.

A real answer beginning in the soprano at measure 2 exploits dominant *of* the dominant harmony for its third beat, and resolution into the dominant chord on the first beat of measure 3 signals the appearance of another answer rather than a link, for which there is no modulatory need since the opening scale degrees are avoided with this third (bass) entry. In Sinfonias One and Eight, where the subject or motive begins on the fifth scale degree and appears in the bass as the third entry--a situation which somewhat parallels the use of an answer also starting on the fifth scale degree in the bass as a third entry--exactly the same structural condition (absence of a link) and harmonic condition (a dominant chord of the dominant, progressing to the dominant) occur, although the third entry in each of these sinfonias appears on the first entry's pitch classes rather than those of the second entry. The two-note bass idea of measure 1 in this E-Major Sinfonia shows up inverted in the alto accompanying the soprano's answer in measure 2 (along with evenly moving dotted quarter notes in the bass), and *un*inverted but transposed, also in the alto, in measure 3, along with the bass's answer, providing invertible counterpoint with the events of measure 1, somewhat in the manner of a countermotive.

The second and third beats of the answer as it is found in the bass (down one octave from the preceding answer in the alto) become the point-of-departure for a four-stage sequence (measures 3-5), and since each stage has a two-beat idea within the prevailing triple compound meter, hemiola results in conjunction with a steady harmonic rhythm involving root movement which flows around the entire diatonic circle of descending fifths. Measures 6-7-8 bring back 2-3-4 with the bass down a perfect fifth and the two upper voices transposed at the lower fifth and upper fourth in such a way that invertible counterpoint results.

The last beat of measure 8 has a chord which is common to E major and C♯ minor, preparing the way for a C♯-minor statement of the opening motive, beginning with the alto's tied D♯ (rather than C♯ to conform to the original plan) and continuing in the relative minor key one scale degree "off." This results in a use of the subtonic (B-natural) within the framework of an *ascending* natural-minor scale fragment--a fairly unusual situation in the *Inventions and Sinfonias* of Bach. The following measure (10) has the soprano imitating the alto from 9, at the seventh, which in this case places the motive on the correct degrees for C♯ minor, although the initial C♯ is treated nonharmonically (as a retardation).

Example 6-1.  Measures 1-11

The passage continues episodically at 11 and after, with groups of disjunct eighth notes relating back to the generating motive, in a rhythmic sense. The first such group is given out by the soprano, which is imitated--after a slightly different upbeat note--at the lower fifth by the alto during the next measure, as the passage moves into B major, and then--at yet another lower fifth (which now includes the upbeat note from the measure before)--by the bass. The bass statement's D# near the end of measure 13 is abbreviated slightly,

in relationship to its predecessors in the other voices,
so that the idea (upbeat note and all) can continue,
still in the bass, in a sequential manner which perpet-
uates one-bar restatement at the lower fifth during measure 14, and further such restatement during 15. All
told, then, there are five statements, one per bar, of
the soprano idea from measure 11, during the passage at
11-15, each statement after the first (strict or free)
down a fifth from the preceding one, in conjunction with
chordal root movement which also descends by fifth for
the most part. Accompanying these presentations are
various thoughts in slower-moving note values which suggest the countermotive.

The first large section of this essentially bi-
partite piece ends with an alto statement conveying most
of the motive at the subdominant level in B major (beginning in measure 16) followed by a freely inverted
statement in the soprano which leads into a perfect
authentic cadence (measures 17-18).

Example 6-2.   Measures 11-18

The second section gets under way in B major with a motive/motive/answer series of entries (in opposition to the first section in E major with its motive/answer/answer series). The bass leads off, mostly unaccompanied (measure 18), followed by the alto with imitation at the octave, as the soprano remains silent and the bass temporarily doubles at the lower sixth before breaking off to provide a suggestion of E major (measure 19). The soprano resumption in measure 20 provides imitation at the fifth, in F# minor, as both underlying voices become less active.

This third entry of the second section in the soprano launches a rising three-stage sequence on the entire answer (as opposed to the third entry of section one in the bass, which launches a *falling four*-stage sequence on two/thirds of the motive), additional stages being found in A major (measure 21) and C# minor (22), the former assisted by the inverted countermotive (from measure 2) in the alto, and the latter, by a freely inverted account of the motive in the bass.

Example 6-3.   Measures 18-23

This inverted bass account in measure 22 gives rise to a passage in which strict accounts of the upside-down motive (in the alto at 23 and bass at 25) alternate with free ones (in the soprano at 24 and alto at 26) in an

imitative manner, accompanied mostly by sustained notes
or rests, except in measure 25, where the soprano has a
certain amount of eighth-note activity along with the
bass. During the course of this passage, the key changes back to E major. Measures 27-28 then bring back the
earlier passage from 4-5 in transposition, with the soprano line down a second and the alto and bass lines
exchanged in invertible counterpoint (the alto line from
before down a ninth here as the bass and the bass line
from before down a second here as the alto). The harmonic sequence of falling fifths thus involves chordal
roots one degree below those of the earlier passage.

Example 6-4.    Measures 23-29

Measure 29 reintroduces the inverted motive in the
bass for a free isolated appearance, after which a series of *un*inverted statements alternate back and forth
between the upper two voice parts, most situated upon
unconventional scale degrees, and each beginning with

the motive's second note: D♯ in the alto in measure 30, C♯ in the soprano in 31, A in the alto (32), and F♯ in the soprano (33), as the bass contributes lone dotted quarter notes on the first beat of each measure. A half cadence set off by a fermata, followed by rests occupying two full compound beats, in all three voice parts, brings the passage to a close in measure 34.

Example 6-5.  Measures 29-34

The inverted motive presented by the soprano in composite rhythm with its prime form by the alto initiates a coda at measure 35, where the bass temporarily continues its one-note-per-bar treatment prior to imitating the alto at the lower fourth (starting with the second note of 36) in a mostly monophonic manner as the other voices fall silent only to resume (37) with the motive (minus its first note in the alto) in contrary motion.

The only sixteenth notes of the piece provide a brief flurry of activity within the framework of a sequence in the soprano, which gets its first one-beat stage under way with the final F♯ of 37. After three complete stages--each starting with a nine-eight suspension--plus the very beginning of a fourth (which commences with a retardation that is displaced downward an octave prior to resolving), the original motive, start-

ing on the submediant rather than the tonic, and ending freely, is brought in by the alto, doubled (after
the first note) in sixths by the soprano.  The sinfonia
concludes with an inperfect authentic cadence following
disjunct eighth notes in the bass (measure 40) somewhat
reminiscent of those in the soprano at measure 11.

Example 6-6.   Measures 35-41

# CHAPTER 7: SINFONIA NUMBER SEVEN (E MINOR)

The E-Minor Sinfonia, like the earlier one in Eb Major (and the later one in G Minor) has a subject in the soprano which, although it begins on the fifth scale degree, does not allow for the use of a tonal answer according to the traditional practice, because unlike most of Bach's sinfonia subjects, it concludes in such a way (on the seventh scale degree--in this case the leading tone) that dominant harmony is called for rather than tonic harmony. In addition to precluding a tonal answer, this feature necessitates a sudden change of mode from the B-*major* chord (the dominant chord in E minor) on beat one of measure 3, directly to the B-*minor* chord (the tonic chord in B minor) on beat two of the same measure, in order to avoid an appearance of the answer in the dominant *major* key (B major), which is not closely related to E minor.

The end of this answer--a real answer at the lower fourth mostly doubled at the upper third by the soprano (a doubling which creates a double suspension across the bar-line into measure 4)--exhibits the same condition, with a sudden mode change from the F♯ major triad (the dominant triad in B minor) on the first beat of measure 5, to the F♯ minor chord (the supertonic chord in E minor) on the second beat, as the alto continues its imitation of the soprano, somewhat canonically, beyond the boundary of the subject, into the first beat of measure 6, still at the lower fourth, and then an additional measure at the lower *fifth*.

The soprano, following its opening statement of the subject (measures 1-3) and its partial doubling of the alto's answer (3-5), provides additional doubling of the alto at the sixth (5-7), thus projecting three successive statements (complete or virtually complete) of the opening idea, each on different scale degrees, during its first six measures. The third statement,

which creates harmonic inversion (invertible counterpoint) between the soprano and alto with the second
statement, belongs to a passage which functions as a link
between the second and third entries of the opening exposition, modulating back to E minor, and exhibiting a
high degree of expressivity resulting from prominent
employment of the diminished seventh chord in addition
to the aforementioned change of mode.

During the first four measures, the bass has much
rhythmic cohesion, supplied by recurrences of a three-
beat rhythmic unit. Its rising fourth from B to E within the last half of measure 1 offers momentary imitation of the soprano line, and this, plus the subsequent
falling second, furnish a configuration during the last
half of measure 1 which has a modified motivic relationship with the rising-third/falling-second configuration
of the subject just after the beginning of the second
measure, as well; but, although this bass configuration
plus the note which follows is found elsewhere, it has
less of a countersubject function than does the sixteenth-note material found later at 14 and after.  The
bass's sixteenth notes of measure 5 relate to the soprano's from 3, first with inversion and then without.

The bass subject found in measures 7-9 at the lower octave with the soprano entry of 1-3 rounds out the
voicing to conclude the opening exposition.  Invertible
counterpoint involving the bass and alto from the middle of measure 7 to the middle of 8 in relationship to
the soprano and bass, respectively, from the middle of
1 to the middle of 2, creates the temporary impression
of a subject/countersubject affiliation, but this effect
is short-lived, as the alto becomes free, in thirds with
the soprano once again, during measure 8.

Example 7-1.　Measures 1-9

A five-measure episode modulating quickly into B minor ensues, initially featuring the last half of the subject with interval expansion creating a rising fourth in lieu of the original rising third into its second note, so that its opening sounds just like the bass idea starting in the last half of measure 1 and continuing into 2. As this line is unfolding in the bass during measures 9-10, the alto imitates its opening portion in stretto at the upper octave, after which the soprano (10-11) presents the same tail portion of the subject with*out* interval expansion, mostly up another third. This soprano account is then taken up by the bass in a slightly ornamental fashion at the lower octave (11-12). Much color is again achieved through conspicuous use of the diminished seventh chord (and diminished triad) as well as the suspension (measures 9 and 12-13).

A final soprano statement of the subject's tail motive, on the appropriate scale degrees for B minor, begins in measure 13 and paves the way for a perfect authentic cadence, the final chord of which necessitates use of a different concluding note for the motive (B, instead of A♯). This cadence, which ends the first section of the sinfonia in the dominant minor key, is preceded by a cadential six-four chord and additionally strengthened by an anticipation that is part of the subject fragment itself.

Example 7-2.  Measures 9-14

Section two instigates the use of almost continuous sixteenth-note motion in one part or another. It begins in just two voices with a two-entry counterexposition, which reverses the voicing procedure of the opening exposition, the alto (measures 14-16) presenting the subject down an octave from where it was originally situated in the soprano, and the soprano (16-18) imitating the alto at the perfect fifth with a real answer at the same pitches originally employed by the alto in measures 3-5. The sixteenth-note bass line--initially derivative (F#, B, A, G) but with rhythmic diminution, from the bass line crossing from measure 1 into 2--has more characteristics of a countersubject than does any material which precedes it, for most of that which is found in conjunction with the alto's subject statement during measures 14-16 shows up in transposition down a fourth during 16-18 in conjunction with the soprano's answer, as well as elsewhere, later in the piece. The alto line of measures 16-17 does not employ doubling procedures like those of the soprano from measures 3-4, but it does bring in the bass motive from 4, at the upper octave, during 17.

Example 7-3.    Measures 14-18

This second section becomes episodic sooner than does the first section because of the absence of a third complete entry of the subject or answer. An altered fragment of the subject's head motive is found doubled in thirds during measure 18 in the bass and alto, accompanied by a modified version of the sixteenth-note countersubject's first one-bar motive (from measure 14), this sixteenth-note thought being then freely imitated, mostly at the lower seventh, by the alto during measure 19, where a two-stage freely sequential passage modulating into D major is inaugurated. The alto, starting with its third sixteenth note of measure 19, begins the first two-bar stage of this sequence, the second stage of which (measures 21-22) is virtually complete, and the soprano slightly later follows suit with the same material, mostly up a ninth, *its* sequence, however, including an initial tied note (F♯). Meanwhile, the bass exploits the *rhythmic* pattern of the subject's first four notes with pitches arranged so as to eliminate all leaps, first right-side-up and then upside-down, as the first stage of a sequence, the second stage of which-- like that of the other voices--appears at the lower second, and is almost but not quite complete.

During measures 23 and 24, as they lead into 25, the bass takes up the sixteenth-note pattern just found in the upper voices, treating it sequentially (from the second note of 23) with two *one*-bar stages, the second down a fifth from the first, as the soprano sustains a subdominant pedal, and the alto temporarily doubles the bass in sixths before becoming less active, prior to the imperfect authentic cadence which concludes this second section of the sinfonia, in D major, the subtonic major key.

Example 7-4.   Measures 18-25

In contrast to section two, which has an extensive

episode, section three--if it is construed as lasting
until the half cadence in measures 36-37--is virtually
*non*-episodic, having one entry after another of the generating idea, six entries in all, occupying twelve measures, although the last three are slightly modified.
The soprano leads off with the first major-key subject
statement of the piece (measures 25-27), accompanied by
the alto with an inverted account of the sixteenth-note
countersubject's first measure (starting on the second
half of the first beat), the last two beats of which
are sequenced at the upper perfect fifth during the
first two beats of measure 26, along with the subject's
continuation.

Like the voice-part supplying the second entry in
section one and section two, the bass remains silent as
the subject with its accompanying material is unfolding, promoting a condition which attracts notice to its
entrance during measures 27-29 at the lower double octave (with a replica of, rather than an answer to, the
preceding soprano subject). The bass is accompanied by
the alto with slow-moving note values and the soprano
with material from the sixteenth-note countersubject's
first measure *uninverted* (measure 27) as the basis for
a sequence which moves down a second (28). Invertible
counterpoint relating measures 27 and 14 (or 16) therefore results, but *not* 28 and 15 (or 17) because of the
absence of strict sequence during the earlier passage.

Following this bass statement of the subject in D
major, another bass statement, which modulates into B
minor, effects a sequence on the entire subject, at the
lower third. As accompaniment to the second stage, the
alto (measure 29) has a fragment of the sixteenth-note
countersubject, and the soprano (30), upside-down and
right-side-up fragments.

Example 7-5.   Measures 25-31

Another pair of sequentially united entries unfolds in the alto during measures 31-35, with interval
expansion downward between the fourth and fifth notes
(from what originally was a second to what here is a
third) assisting a modulation downward by degree, from B
minor to A minor during the first stage, and from A minor to G, during the second stage. The bass and soprano lines are also sequential, the bass (freely so)
doubling the alto at the lower sixth during the last
portion of each stage, and the soprano having constant-
ly moving sixteenth notes which encompass material from
the sixteenth-note countersubject's first measure right-
side-up during the first half of each stage (measures
31 and 33) and the same material upside-down during the
second half (measures 32 and 34).

A final entry of this section appears in the bass
during measures 35-37, starting on staff degrees which
suggest D minor, but initially harmonized in G minor--a
non closely related key that results from mode change
brought about by the use of Eb (which, along with a subsequent A, creates a melodic augmented fourth) and Bb
in the soprano--and concluding in E minor. The appropriate degrees for the tonic key emerge as a consequence
of interval expansion into the entry's sixth note, where
a rising fourth (E to A) supplants what originally was
a rising third. The alto's doubling at the third creates harmonic inversion with the events between the same
pair of voices in measures 32 and 34. The soprano retains the same two-bar sixteenth-note idea it has been
using, with the first bar (35) manipulated somewhat by
interval adjustment which produces partial transposition (in relationship to what happens in 33) and the
second bar (36)--after its first two notes--strict (in
relationship to what happens in 34) except for transposition down a third from G minor to E minor (Example
7-6).

Example 7-6.   Measures 31-37

Measures 37-39 return the original subject in the soprano, just as it is found at the beginning, contributing temporary relief from the incessant sixteenth-note motion. The middle portion of the bass line from measures 1-2 also comes back here, at the lower octave, but the slight imitative effect the bass purveys with the soprano is overshadowed by the alto, which imitates a more sizeable chunk of the bass line, doubling the soprano subject's final portion at the lower third and then the lower sixth, as it does.

Example 7-7.   Measures 37-39

Just after the tied note at the beginning of measure 39, material based on the sixteenth-note countersubject's initial measure is set into motion by the bass as the first part of a threefold statement, the second

part relating to the first sequentially at the lower
fifth, and the third part transposed down an additional
third.   The alto and soprano, after having assisted in
the process of tonicizing the subdominant chord (measures 39 and 40), emphasize the subdominant further by
presenting false (incomplete) entries of the opening
idea starting on E (the subdominant's fifth degree): E,
A, B, C, in stretto (40-41).   The second of these two
entries, in the soprano during measure 41, is accompanied by eighth notes from below in the alto, which having finished *its* false entry, continues with a transposed version of the bass motive from the end of measure 1 and the beginning of 2, as part of an ascending
horn-fifth pattern with the soprano.

Fragments from the sixteenth-note countersubject
outlast fragments from the subject, as the soprano's
false entry dissipates in measure 42.   Brief sixteenth-
note imitation by the alto at the end of 42 sets up two
suspensions, the first of which is highly ornamented,
in the soprano, leading to the final cadence, a perfect
authentic cadence which employs a Picardy third.

Example 7-8.   Measures 39-44

CHAPTER 8:  SINFONIA NUMBER EIGHT (F MAJOR)


Three well-defined sections approximately equal in
length (measures 1-7, 7-15, and 15-23), each concluding
with a perfect authentic cadence, constitute the overall design of the F-Major Sinfonia.  Section one contains an exposition having the traditional plan of one
entry for each voice (measures 1-4), a brief, one-and-
one-half-bar episode (4-5), and a subject entry in the
dominant major key (5-6) plus upper-octave imitation
(6-7), the final note of which provides a third for the
cadence's tonic chord.

The alto initiates the subject during measure 1 as
a one-bar idea within the range of a perfect fifth, having changing tones within its fourth beat. This subject
is accompanied in the bass by a simple, slow-moving,
syncopated idea, the recurrent portion of which (F, E, F),
starts on the second beat as a countersubject.  Since
the subject begins on the fifth scale degree and ends
on the third, the answer is adjusted tonally, so that
its first note imitates the first note of the subject
at the upper fourth, with F (which fits the tonic harmony outlined by the other two voices) instead of G
(which does not), but the remainder of the answer is
real (imitating at the upper fifth).  The alto's countersubject exhibits closer spacing beneath this answer
than does the bass's countersubject beneath the subject
during measure 1, and the bass of measure 2 provides a
thought which largely moves in shared rhythm with the
soprano line.

As with Sinfonia Number One--the only other sinfonia having a subject that begins on the fifth scale degree and ends on the third--a true modulation is not
employed with the answer, but rather only simulated by
means of a dominant chord of the dominant on the final
beat of measure 2; therefore, no passage is needed to
serve as a link for modulatory purposes to bring back

65

the tonic key, and immediately upon the conclusion of the second entry at the beginning of measure 3, the third entry starts in the bass, with dominant harmony instead of tonic harmony, as at the beginning. This dominant harmony creates a free tone (a fairly rare nonharmonic tone in Bach's contrapuntal works--one that is approached and left by leap) out of the bass subject's second note (A), in addition to changing tones out of the soprano's F and D, as the soprano sequences the tail portion of its answer from the fourth beat of measure 2 prior to taking up the countersubject. The countersubject's appearance above the subject here, in relationship to its previous appearances below the subject and answer, results in invertible counterpoint.

Example 8-1.   Measures 1-4

The ensuing episode (during measure 4 and the first half of 5) employs sequence in all three voices, with the soprano and alto sharing material--the subject's first three notes (the final one elongated)--as they engage in an imitative dialogue, and the bass employing somewhat less derivative material. A modulation into C major takes place soon after this episode has begun, but the tonic chord is avoided, as the passage unfolds with harmonic as well as melodic sequence.

The bass then brings in a C-major statement of the subject (starting in the last half of measure 5), following which the alto imitates the bass at the upper octave, concluding section one. The countersubject is not used with the bass statement, although syncopation,

one of its characteristic features, is exhibited by the
alto, which presents two ornamented suspensions, each
exploiting a change of bass with its resolution.   In
conjunction with the subsequent alto imitation, however,
the countersubject *is* used, on top, where it strengthens
the cadence, contributing to a welcome release of the
tension which has built up as a consequence of the melodic and harmonic conditions found during measures 4,
5, and 6, as well as the beginning of 7.

Example 8-2.   Measures 4-7

        Section two is saturated with statements of the
subject or answer in various keys, starting with the
dominant major.   It begins with a passage in canon between the soprano and bass, as the alto falls silent,
allowing this special device of imitation to stand out
unencumbered, in the polar voices.   The soprano leads
off with a complete statement of the subject suffixed
by an additional note (D) and followed by transposition
down a third, minus the additional note.

        Meanwhile, the bass has begun imitating at the low-
er twelfth (both perfect and imperfect) after just one
beat, spawning a very tight overlapping condition and
remaining strict--except on the first half of the fourth
beat in measure 9--until the middle of 10, where a three-
voice texture resumes.   The bass imitation's first subject statement does not--like the soprano's--employ the
original scale degrees as applied to C major, but it
does, following the re-introduction of Bb in measure 8,
end on the original degrees for F major, through which

this passage temporarily passes on its way to D minor. Conversely, the second soprano statement (measures 8-9) does not utilize the original degrees as applied to F major *or* D minor, but the second *bass* statement does, for D minor, although it concludes on the first degree rather than the third, near the end of measure 9, momentarily liberating the bass voice from its canonical obligation.

A third soprano statement, from the middle of 9 to the middle of 10, breaks the sequential interval of transposition but (like the bass one just before) employs the original fifth scale degree of the current key (D minor) as a starting point. Canonical imitation of this statement by the bass is incomplete, and the soprano's F# in lieu of F-natural on the third beat of measure 10 directs the passage into G minor at about the point where the canon ends.

Example 8-3.  Measures 7-10

The alto then re-enters with the subject starting on the fifth degree in G minor (measures 10-11) accompanied by both bass and soprano, the latter with the countersubject, which was avoided during the canonical passage with its focus upon a two-voice texture. The bass, after having supplied the subject's opening *rhythmic* scheme during the initial part of measure 11, takes up the subject, itself, during the latter part of 11, by imitating the alto from the previous measure at the lower double octave, still in G minor to start out with. Along with the first portion of this bass entry (during the last half of 11 as it leads into 12), the soprano simulates the countersubject, while the alto provides a compressed statement of the subject (its first three notes--starting on Bb--overlapping its last five, in a different transposition).

The bass (measures 12-13) proceeds to supply a ton-

al answer to its own subject (as well as the alto subject which precedes it), as the passage moves into D
minor, after which the soprano (13-14) presents a *real*
answer in the same key, underlaid by the alto with countersubject material and doubled by the bass, first at
the lower tenth, then the lower sixth, before the bass
becomes free to pave the way for a deceptive harmonic
progression which coincides with the end of the real answer in the middle of 14. The submediant chord of this
progression on beat three introduces a passage in which
there are no intact statements of the subject or answer,
only bits and pieces, the most derivative of which are
two-note fragments taken freely from the subject's opening, found with attached material mostly in the bass
during the last half of 14 and first half of 15. A perfect authentic cadence reinforced by an anticipation on
its dominant chord but softened by a four-three suspension on its tonic chord brings this second section to a
close in the middle of 15.

Example 8-4.  Measures 10-15

Section three continues the episodic passage from
the very end of section two, its transitional character
intensified by modulations into F major in measure 16
and Bb major in 17. The subject's first three notes
with interval expansion (from a fourth to a sixth between the second and third notes) and also in their o-
riginal form, dominate this passage initially, being
used in an imitative-sequential manner reminiscent of

what happens at measures 4-5, but freely.

The alto opens this section with a falling-third/ rising-sixth pattern, responded to by the soprano with the original falling-third/rising-fourth, which is found again in the alto and soprano during measure 16, in transposition. The intervalically expanded version is reaffirmed by the soprano near the end of 16 (starting on C) and followed by the original version once again, doubled in tenths between the bass and alto. One final appearance of this three-note configuration ensues in the soprano during measure 17.

Example 8-5.   Measures 15-17

The last note of this appearance, the soprano's Eb, is held over as a suspension into the third beat of measure 17, and its resolution begins a process in which the soprano doubles the alto at the upper sixth throughout a complete statement of the subject in Bb major as the bass sustains a tonic pedal. Certain devices created by these events, such as the pedal six-four chord (on beat four of measure 17) and double changing tones (within beat two of measure 18) sustain interest during this moment of convergence where there is less contrapuntal independence than there is elsewhere in the piece.

The soprano sequences itself at the upper third starting in the middle of 18. In doing so, it also imitates the alto at the upper octave, and it is, in turn, imitated in stretto by the bass, which employs the same time interval (one beat) and pitch interval (the lower twelfth) of imitation as that employed during the canonical passage at measure 7 and after. The bass imitation becomes slightly free due to interval expansion within the third beat of measure 19 (Example 8-6).

The last half of measure 19 reintroduces the earlier passage starting during the *first* half of measure

Example 8-6.  Measures 17-19

4, in transposition (essentially from C major there to
F major here).  The bass (beginning with beat four of
measure 19) adheres to its  line from before (beginning
with beat two of measure 4) at the upper perfect fourth
for better than two measures,  and the upper voices are
exchanged in invertible counterpoint at the octave, the
alto being strict with the soprano from before at the
lower perfect fifth,  and the soprano being strict with
the alto from before  at the upper perfect fourth, both
for approximately three measures.  The closing portion
of section three,  therefore,  strikingly resembles the
corresponding portion of section one; however, the subject in counterpoint with its  countersubject does not
provide the final event of section three  as  it does of
section one, for additional beats have been added (measure 23), rounding out the passage and contributing nonharmonic devices (suspensions and an anticipation) which
lend finality to the conclusion of the sinfonia.

Example 8-7.  Measures 19-23

# CHAPTER 9:  SINFONIA NUMBER NINE (F MINOR)

Like the D-Major Sinfonia (Number Three), the one
in F Minor employs a subject and *two* countersubjects.
In minor keys, as within the opening exposition, the
subject uses nine of the twelve possible tones (more
than any other sinfonia subject); countersubject one, all
six pitches embracing the upper tetrachord (and occasionally one more); and countersubject two, *ten* of the twelve
tones. (Major mode applied to the subject and countersubject two reduces slightly the number of different
pitches used). Furthermore, pitches have been arranged
so as to create an augmented fourth within the subject,
two augmented primes (chromatic half-steps) within countersubject one, and--in minor keys only--two diminished
thirds as well as an augmented second within countersubject two. Since countersubject one shows up with
every statement of the subject or answer, and countersubject two, with every statement except for the first,
and since subject- or countersubject-derived material
also shows up in links and episodes, an unusually large
number of augmented and diminished melodic intervals
(in addition to cross relations) may be found throughout the sinfonia, which has certain areas of tonal in-
stability as a consequence of its chromatic approach.

As might be expected, triple (invertible, three-
part) counterpoint results from the frequent association of these three independent and distinctive musical
ideas; however, only four of the six possibilities for
inversion have been realized (as opposed to the six possibilities realized within the D-Major Sinfonia). Triple counterpoint is also featured in certain episodic
passages.

The subject--a two-bar idea broken up by rests in
a fashion not found with the other sinfonia subjects or
motives--is given over to a rising two-stage sequence
during its first measure and an abrupt leap that reach-

es from the subdominant above to the leading tone, followed by upward resolution and then conjunct movement
down a portion of the natural minor scale, during its
second measure. The subject is located in the alto o-
ver a countersubject which starts with the bass's second note--countersubject one, easily identified, here
and in all subsequent appearances, by its quarter-note
descent filling in a perfect fourth with diatonic and
chromatic half steps (from F, the tonic, to C, the dominant), during measures 1-2. This descending line is
suffixed with a series of even eighth notes followed by
a longer note whenever it is given to the bass (measures
1-3, 11-13, and 33-35), but by a syncopated configuration whenever it is given to an upper voice (measures
3-5, 7-9, 13-15, 18-20, 24-26, 26-28, and 31-33), and
it tends to fit the subject and answer in a manner that
causes the middle eighth-note of each three-note group
to function as an appoggiatura, even measure 1's Ab (nonharmonic to the implied supertonic seventh chord in third
inversion) and Bb (nonharmonic to the implied leading-
tone or dominant seventh chord of the subdominant), both
of which are more consonant than the notes which follow
them.

A real answer at the upper perfect fifth in the
soprano, pivoting almost immediately into C minor, responds to this alto subject. The answer is accompanied
in the alto by countersubject one, transposed up a perfect twelfth so that it underlies the answer more closely than it does when it appears in the bass with the
subject just before, and employing the new (syncopated)
tail motive (which resembles a distorted version of the
subject's head). Beneath the answer in the soprano and
first countersubject in the alto, the bass introduces
a second countersubject that is much more active rhythmically than either of the two melodic lines associated
with it contrapuntally. During the last half of measure
4, it takes over the even-eighth-note time values--but
not the pitches--of the bass from the last half of measure 2. Although this second countersubject is even
more elaborate than the subject in terms of its pitch
content, it avoids the chromatic half step which is employed so conspicuously with countersubject one, supplanting it to some extent with the diminished third as
a melodic interval (beat three of measure 3 and beat
one of measure 4), the two pitches of which are followed by the intervening pitch--Ab, F#, G, and Db, B,
C, respectively (Example 9-1).

A two-bar link modulating through the Neapolitan
chord in C minor (which becomes the submediant in F mi-

Example 9-1. Measures 1-5

nor) on beat three of measure 5, follows the answer. This link begins in the soprano with the subject's first three notes modified by means of interval contraction, followed at the end of the measure by a sixteenth-note grouping which with chromatically altered changing tones separated by the interval of a diminished third, suggests a portion of the first motive from countersubject two, metrically displaced. This, as a one-measure unit in the soprano, is imitated by the alto at the lower fifth, with a one-beat time interval which creates a canonical effect, as the bass drops out leaving just a two-voice texture. As the imitation is ending, the soprano becomes more disjunct, taking up a two-beat thought that is treated sequentially and leads into the third entry of the exposition. The alto, instead of continuing canonically at the lower fifth, simply restates most of its last half-bar idea a fourth down, during the third and fourth beats of measure 6, causing an imitative rehash of the soprano line from the fourth beat of measure 5 and the first beat of 6, at the lower octave.

The bass entry which completes the opening exposition during measures 7-9 is a subject located down an octave from the original alto subject and down a perfect twelfth from the soprano's answer. It is accompanied by countersubject one (with the syncopated tail) in the soprano, up a perfect fourth from where it was

situated in the alto during measures 3-5, and most of
countersubject two (the less active closing portion is
free), up an octave plus a fourth, then--because of octave displacement which does away with the octave interval between countersubject two's first and second
segments--just a fourth. Invertible counterpoint therefore is produced between measures 7-9 and 3-5, the two
countersubjects being inverted with the subject (answer) but not each other.  According to a letter symbology which identifies the melodic lines from top to
bottom as ABC during measures 3-5, those at 7-9 can be
identified as BCA.

Example 9-2.  Measures 5-9

Measures 9-10 comprise a brief episode separating
the entries of the opening exposition from an additional entry in Ab major, which concludes the first section
of the sinfonia.  During the first measure of this episode, the alto presents the first half of the subject,
sequence and all, with interval expansion into the second note of each three-note group, while the soprano
initiates an idea, part of which is imitated a half bar
later by the bass at the lower perfect twelfth.  During
the second measure of this passage (10), the alto imitates the soprano from the first measure (9) at the lower perfect fifth, and the soprano--after one beat--imi-
tates the alto at the upper eleventh (then fourth), creating invertible counterpoint over the same bass mate-

rial (starting with the second beat) up a fourth.

This episode, which passes through Bb minor and also Eb, on its way to Ab major, is followed by an Ab-major statement of the subject (measures 11-12) in the
alto, accompanied by countersubject one in the bass and
countersubject two (again exhibiting octave displacement between its first and second segments, and again
ending freely) in the soprano, so countersubject two is
now presented in invertible counterpoint with both the
subject and countersubject one (in relationship to the
passage at measures 3-5 where all three ideas are found
together for the first time). The resulting top-to-
bottom lettering scheme is thus CAB. Major mode reduces the number of different pitches used with the subject from nine to seven (those of the Ab major diatonic
scale) and those used with countersubject two, from ten
to nine, doing away with all of the latter's diminished
and augmented intervals in the process and creating a
different approach to tonicization; countersubject one,
however, retains its original pitch format exactly, and
this fixed condition spawns a borrowed chord (beat two
of measure 12), which offsets the bright quality resulting from the employment of secondary dominants earlier within the subject statement by creating a darken-
ing effect prior to the cadence which concludes section
one.

Example 9-3.  Measures 9-13

Section two begins with a soprano entry of the subject which initially reflects Eb minor (although the
underlying harmonic/tonal conditions are somewhat tenu-
ous) and ends in Eb *major*, thus causing it to serve--in
a sense--as an answer to the preceding subject in Ab
major, even though the two are separated by a fairly
definitive-sounding cadence. With countersubject one
(having the syncopated tail motive) in the middle, and
countersubject two (still characterized by octave displacement) on the bottom, the same distribution of voices found with the second entry (measures 3-5) is employed.

Example 9-4.   Measures 13-15

During the ensuing three-bar episode, modulations
take place, most notably into F minor and C minor. First
the soprano and bass (15-16), then alto and bass (16-18)
engage in an imitative dialogue involving the beginning
three notes of the subject exploiting three sequential
stages (rather than two, as in the subject, itself),
that rise by second. The bass version which appears in
dialogue with the alto's, applies octave displacement
to the second and third notes of each stage. The remaining material--in the alto during measures 15-16 and
transposed in the soprano during 16-17--makes use of
quarter notes which (starting on the weak beat) are sequential in half-bar units too, and which in groups
of threes (also starting on the weak beat) formulate
the subject's first three notes in retrograde inversion
and rhythmic augmentation. Imitation (with a six-beat
time interval) of the soprano by the alto at the lower
fourth, and of the alto by the soprano at the upper
fifth produces invertible counterpoint at the octave
between these two voice parts from one three-stage sequential grouping to the next during measures 15-17 (Example 9-5).

Rounding out section two is a C-minor statement of

Example 9-5.   Measures 15-18

the subject by the alto, accompanied by countersubject
one (with the syncopated tail motive) in the soprano,
and countersubject two (in its complete, original form,
*with* the upward octave leap between its first and second segments) in the bass, so the subject and countersubject one are inverted with each other (from measures
3-5) over the same bass line (down an octave), although
this inversion is momentarily cancelled out during measure 19 by voice crossing. From top to bottom, the symbology for most of this passage, therefore, is BAC.

Example 9-6.   Measures 18-20

     The first two measures of the four-measure episode
which begins in measure 20 obviously relate back to the
two measures constituting the brief episode at 9-10,
the soprano part here being strict with the soprano
part from before at the lower perfect fourth, the alto,
with the bass from before at the upper perfect fifth,
and the bass (except for one eighth-note, on the second
half of the first beat), with the alto from before at
the lower perfect eleventh. The consequence of this
rearranged recurrence is invertible counterpoint involving the material of the lower two voices, and since similar exchange took place *between* measures 9 and 10 with
the upper two voices and now takes place between 20
and 21 among all three of the voices, four of the six

possibilities for distribution of this episodic material in triple counterpoint have been realized (tempered
slightly by crossing of voices on beat three of measure
21 in a manner similar to that at 19).   This latter episode is twice as long as the earlier one upon which it
is based, because it uses the two-measure unit as the
first stage of a sequence, the second stage of which is
strict at the lower major second in the soprano, virtually strict at the same interval in the alto, and strict
except for octave displacement in the bass, which has
the first three notes of its second stage (starting on
the last half of the first beat in measure 22) at the
upper minor seventh with those of the first stage, and
the remainder at the lower major second.   Tonal insta-
bility manifested by the episode at 9-11 is compounded
here at 20-24 by the greater length, and this latter
passage touches fleetingly upon *several* different keys
as it leads from C minor to Db major.

Example 9-7.   Measures 20-24

Measures 24-26 then bring forth the subject in Db
major in the bass, in counterpoint with countersubject
one (having the syncopated tail again) in the soprano,
and countersubject two (having *its* tail shaped as in
measures 8-9) in the alto, touching off the same voicing arrangement employed during measures 7-9.   A harmonic scheme employing tonicizations like those found
with the earlier major-key subject statement at 11-13
is applied here.

The soprano entry at 26-28, in Ab major, stands in much the same type of answer relationship to the subject that precedes it as does the entry at 13-15 to the subject that precedes *it*, and the musical conditions of these two passages are identical except for transposition up a perfect fourth in the upper two voices and down a perfect fifth in the bass--until the second beat of 27, where octave displacement, which now occurs between countersubject two's second and third segments, in relationship to the statement at 13-15, brings the bass transposition in line with that of the upper voices.

Example 9-8.   Measures 24-28

During measures 28-33, the soprano brings back the alto line from 15-20 up a perfect fourth, almost exactly, the alto brings back the soprano line down a perfect fifth, and the bass brings back its own line mostly up a perfect fourth (or eleventh, as the case may be), so both the episode from measures 15-18 and the subject/countersubject entries from 18-20 are returned here with the upper two voices exchanged in invertible counterpoint. Measures 31-33 offer some effect of return, albeit rather late, because the subject is found here in the tonic key for the first time since the opening exposition (accompanied by the two countersubjects with the ABC top-to-bottom arrangement first used back in measures 3-5), and this effect of return is intensified by what happens during the final three measures of the

piece, where the middle voice imitates the soprano from
just before at the lower octave, the bass projects countersubject one exactly as it is found at the opening of
the piece, and the soprano presents countersubject two
with the original upward octave leap into its second
segment, but with octave displacement downward into its
final segment. The resulting CAB distribution of voices causes this passage that concludes the piece to be
highly reminiscent of the passage at 11-13 that concludes section one, even to the extent of confirming
the soprano version of countersubject two's tail motive
from the end of measure 12, here at the end of 34, with
an additional anticipation that completes a cambiata-
type melodic configuration (Ab, G, E, F), just prior to
the last chord of the final cadence, a perfect authentic cadence exhibiting the ending note of the alto's
subject as a Picardy third.

Example 9-9.   Measures 28-35

CHAPTER 10:   SINFONIA NUMBER TEN (G MAJOR)


This agreeable little piece is noteworthy, even a-
mong the *Sinfonias*, for the remarkable economy of means
it achieves through manipulation and recycling of motivic material from the subject, as well as the use of
complete, slightly modified subject statements to ful-
fill linking and episodic functions. The opening exposition, for example, has a statement of the subject in
the soprano (measures 1-3) followed by a real answer in
the alto (3-5) and a link of equal length (5-7) in which
the soprano presents another entry, with an elongated
initial note, on the same staff degrees as those employed by the alto with the preceding answer, up an octave (somewhat in the manner of a redundant entry before the fact), but with C-natural in measure 6 supplanting what was C♯ in 4 (and D at the beginning of 7
supplanting F♯ from the beginning of 5), this C-natural
tying in with a modulation from D major, key of the answer, back to G major for the subsequent entry. Both
subject and answer begin on the second half of the first
beat, creating a slightly syncopated effect, and stress
ascending and descending conjunct motion, particularly
the latter--from the sixth degree to the fifth degree a
ninth below--during the second measure.

Four even quarter notes from that portion of the
bass line which starts at measure 2 are slightly recurrent, in transposition (at 4-5 and 21-22), but not
sufficiently so to be considered part of a true countersubject. The soprano doubles the alto at the upper
sixth during the initial portion of the alto's entry in
measure 3 (after which it too instigates a line which
recurs later, at 20-22 and 31-33), and the alto doubles
the soprano at the *lower* sixth during the second half
of measure 5, continuing an extended chain of unbroken
ascending scalewise pitches within a thinner, two-voice
texture, which results from the bass's silence after
the first beat. These doubling practices are reminis-

83

cent of those at the corresponding locations in the E-Minor Sinfonia (Number Seven), which also employs the entire generating idea of the piece (although transposed to scale degrees that do not duplicate those of the subject or answer) as the principal thought of a link between the second and third entries. Doubling at the lower sixth continues in measure 6--one of the germ measures of this piece--on an every-other-pitch basis, generating a series of eighth notes in falling thirds followed by a rising sixth that creates voice crossing.

Example 10-1.   Measures 1-7

The bass statement which, minus its final note, rounds out the opening exposition is accompanied by subject fragments in the upper voices during measure 7. During measure 8, the soprano brings back the alto line from measure 6, up a fourth, creating--along with the subject's continuation in the bass--invertible counter-

point with the events of measure 6; however, expansion
upon these events is provided by the presence of the alto (below which the soprano temporarily crosses) with
its line consisting of a sustained note followed by a
transposed retrograde of the subject's third beat. Measure 8, in turn, provides the basis for 9 and 10 (plus
several other measures throughout the piece: 16, 17,
18, 19, 27, 28, 29, and 30), by setting off a sequential episode with stages falling by second in all three
voice-parts, as the passage modulates into E minor pri-
or to a dominant-to-tonic harmonic progression which
has a sectionalizing effect.

Example 10-2. Measures 7-11

The piece continues at measure 11 with a metrically displaced account of the subject's first seven notes
in the bass starting on E, followed very quickly by an
alto statement of the entire subject, except for an abbreviated initial note and an altered final note. This
alto statement, which temporarily provides stretto at
the octave with the preceding bass line, is characterized not only by minor mode, in contrast to all previous statements, but also by a modulation (into A minor)--up a fourth, as with the entry found during the
link at measures 5-7. This version of the subject is
then imitated at the upper fourth (measures 13-15) by
the soprano, also in minor mode but without an answer-
ing modulation. The bass's eighth-note line accompanying the first part of this soprano entry within measure

13 relates to the subject's third beat through melodic inversion and rhythmic augmentation.  It shows up again within measure 15 in the alto.

Example 10-3.   Measures 11-15

Another statement of the subject is presented during measures 15-16, *not* by the bass, as might be expected to round out the voicing scheme, but rather by the soprano again, up an octave from the alto entry of 11-13, and with a last-minute modulation back to E minor, which results in a late start for the subject, on its second note, which here is the subtonic (D), touching off a cross relation with the bass, as the bass affirms the tonality of E minor (with D♯). Measure 16 relates back to measure 8, with the voices exchanged in invertible counterpoint, so that the material comprising the second bar of the subject itself now lies *above* rather than beneath the other two lines.  A lettering

plan of ABC to identify the individual melodic lines
from top to bottom in measure 8 can be changed to CAB
to identify these same lines in measure 16, which--like
measure 8--becomes the point-of-departure for a sequential episode (measures 16-19), but with one additional
stage. This episode modulates through D major into B
minor and leads to a statement of the subject by the
alto--one having a lengthened initial note (as at measure 5) in the mediant minor key. Its second measure
(21) relates back to measure 4 (originally measure 2 in
the bass) in all three voice parts, and the statement
concludes with a perfect authentic cadence at the beginning of measure 22.

Example 10-4.  Measures 15-22

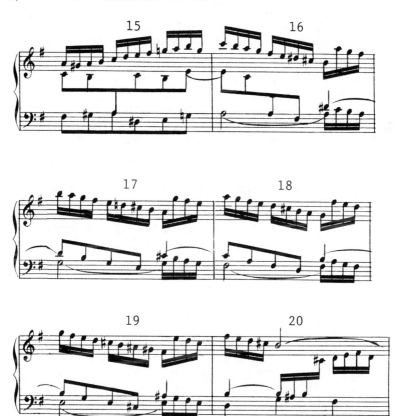

The next section begins with what is probably best interpreted as an episode because of modifications applied to the subject material found in the bass and also because of the sequential manner in which it is employed, with two, two-measure stages at 22-23/24-25. This material starts in B minor (on B) at the beginning of measure 22 (again with an elongated first note) but modulates almost immediately into A minor, accommodating this change of key downward one degree with interval expansion from a third to a fourth between the two descending sixteenth notes at the very end of 22. After the initial note of 23, which is free, the subject resumes and completes itself on the correct scale degrees for A minor, but moves downward rather than upward into measure 24, to generate the sequence's second stage. Since this second stage behaves exactly like the first, it provides an interesting way for the piece to get back into the tonic key, by modulating down another degree from A minor to G major. The alto is sequential in conjunction with the bass throughout this entire four-bar passage (22-26), with material that is partially derivative from the subject's opening portion and then momentarily doubles the soprano's eighth-note line (which relates to the subject in fragmentary form and rhythmic augmentation) at the point where this line too becomes sequential.

Example 10-5.   Measures 22-26

In lieu of a third modulating stage to the bass
sequence, a G-major statement of the subject--unmodi-
fied except for the length of its initial note and pitch
of its final note--is presented by the *alto*, institut-
ing a return. The first measure of this alto statement
(26) has an eighth-note bass line in rising thirds, one
which relates to the falling-third line displayed so
prominently elsewhere in this piece, through inversion.
The second measure (27), like its predecessor at 16,
gives rise to a sequential episode having not only second and third stages (28 and 29), but a fourth one as
well (30). A lettering symbology of B' for the soprano
and C for the alto at 27-30, in relationship to ABC from
top to bottom for measures 8-10 and CAB for 16-19 seems
fitting, although B' as a melodic line has been metrically displaced to the left (earlier in time) by one
beat in relationship to B (and also transposed to a
different location within the scale--up a fifth). The
A material from both previous episodes is only *suggested* during the beginning portion of measure 27 and each
of the following measures based upon it.

Example 10-6. Measures 26-31

Measures 31-33 provide one more brief moment of invertible counterpoint (except where voice crossing occurs, on the third beat of 32) by bringing back transposed soprano and alto material from the end of measure 3 and after, respectively in the alto and soprano. The final tonic-key statement of the subject--since it ends on the third degree, like many of Bach's sinfonia subjects, and is projected by the soprano--creates an *imperfect* authentic cadence for the conclusion.

Example 10-7.   Measures 31-33

# CHAPTER 11:  SINFONIA NUMBER ELEVEN (G MINOR)

An extremely succinct exposition--the most condensed of all the *Sinfonias*, occupying an unusually small percentage of the piece--gets the G-Minor Sinfonia under way in three/eight meter with a one-measure (five-note) motive mostly outlining the tonic triad in the soprano, an answer imitating at the fifth (lower fourth) in the alto, a one-measure link, and a restatement of the motive in the bass with imitation at the lower octave. The motive's opening statement begins on the fifth scale degree but ends on the seventh (subtonic), so a real answer is called for (as in Sinfonias Five and Seven, which also have generating ideas that begin on the fifth degree and end on the seventh, although the seventh in both cases is the leading tone) rather than a tonal answer.

The falling-third bass line of measure 1 continues in measure 2 with a rising sixth, which has the same relationship (displaced at the octave) to the answer that the falling third has to the initial motive, although the dominant key is not really established by this event. The answer's ending has been embellished in such a way that C, its final note, comes at the end, rather than the beginning of measure 3 (which otherwise appears to function as a link) and continues into the starting point of the bass entry as the ornamented resolution of the seventh of a seventh chord in first inversion. At this point (measure 4) the same C serves to prepare the dissonant tone of a suspension, the resolution of which is also ornamented, creating the second stage of an alto sequence in contrapuntal association with the bass motive. The bass line then continues in measure 5 as the alto line continues in measure 3, conveying an idea that provides the rhythmic (but not the melodic) basis for the soprano line of measures 6 and 7, where two more suspensions are located (an ornamented two-one suspension, with voice crossing, and

an *un*ornamented four-three suspension, respectively) pri-
or to a cadential progression at measures 7-8.

Example 11-1.   Measures 1-8

A regrouping takes place at measure 8, which inaugurates a passage having a series of statements--both
unmodified and modified--of the generating motive, one
right after another, or, in some cases, one overlapping
another. The bass reintroduces this motive on its o-
riginal pitch classes, but its ending F-natural in measure 9 is treated differently from a harmonic stand-
point than was the soprano's F-natural in measure 2,
for a chromatic modulation into C minor causes it to
function as the seventh of a dominant seventh chord
(rather than the third of a minor triad, as before).

The alto, meanwhile, brings in a version of the
motive stretched out over the better part of three measures (9-10-11) because of its elongated penultimate
note (G), in imitation of the bass at the upper oc-
tave--which is not entirely perfect, because the prevailing key mandates the use of B-natural in response
to the preceding Bb. The bass, in turn, provides a less
exaggeratedly extended account of the motive (10-11) on
its conventional scale degrees, as applied to C minor,
although its ending note is now a leading tone rather
than a subtonic. This is followed by three additional
accounts which employ interval contraction into the penultimate note: one starting on D in the soprano (measure 11, where the *bass* now has a suspension); one on

G, a perfect fifth down, in the alto (12); and one on
C, another perfect fifth down, in the bass (13), as the
passage modulates into Bb major, the relative major key.
At measure 14, the pattern continues, after a fashion,
with a soprano statement starting on F--the equivalent
of another perfect fifth down, but displaced upward by
two octaves. This statement has its fifth rather than
fourth note adjusted intervalically as the result of an
abrupt leap down to the third of a cadential six-four
chord. The ensuing rhythmic configuration launched by
a dotted note--one of several such rhythmic configurations (the most recent ones being found in the soprano
at 13 and bass at 14)--uses pitches that form a retrograde inversion with those found at measures 3, 4, and
5, giving rise to an escape tone prior to the perfect
authentic cadence concluding this section.

Example 11-2.   Measures 8-16

This treatment, which involves about one motive
statement per bar, continues at measure 16 as the new
section begins with an intervalically contracted version in the bass like earlier versions at 11 and after
in all three voices. This is imitated first at the upper sixth by the alto (measure 17) then up an additional
eleventh by the soprano, which has a two-bar unit at
17-18 that is restated in transposition down a second
except for the final note during 19-20, and down another second--again, except for the final note--during 21-

22.  The bass has two, two-measure units (17-18/19-20)
which are sequential in conjunction with the soprano's
*almost* sequential units, and the alto, engaging in a
freely imitative dialogue with the soprano, is likewise
sequential (18-19/20-21), as the passage modulates into
D minor, the dominant minor key.  The soprano line's
last portion (starting with E in measure 22) then generates its own shorter sequence, with one-bar stages,
concluding this one-entrance-per-bar treatment for the
time being.

Example 11-3.  Measures 16-24

At measure 24, the bass settles into a dominant
pedal which is sustained for several measures before
being temporarily taken over by the alto (measure 29),
and above this pedal in the alto, bass material from
the link at measure 3 is employed sequentially, first
right-side-up (measures 24-25) then upside-down (26-27-
28).  The soprano material of this passage is based upon
a modified account of the opening motive in inversion,
and it too is treated sequentially, first in a free
manner (24-25) and then more strictly (starting with
the second sixteenth note of 26).

The right-side-up soprano statement of the opening
motive which follows in measure 29 is contracted intervalically, like earlier statements at 11-13 and 16-18,

arpeggiating the dominant *seventh* chord rather than just the simple dominant triad in D minor; therefore, although it begins one staff degree higher than the statement at the very beginning of the sinfonia, its last two pitches are the same, setting off a miniature return at measures 30-31-32, which bring back 2-3-4, with the bass mostly at the lower octave. Measure 33, however, parts company with 5, reaffirming D minor--following a brief tonicization of and resolution to the submediant triad (31-32)--through the diminished seventh chord on its leading tone, the first three notes of which in the soprano invert the opening motive's first three notes. A somewhat unusual diminished fourth (F above C#) as the dissonant note of a four-three suspension in the alto sets up one more uninverted presentation of the motive with a modified ending before the concluding chords of the section. Some freedom with the voice leading occurs during measure 34, where a temporarily doubled leading tone (C#) produces interrupted parallel unisons between the alto and bass.

Example 11-4.   Measures 24-36

The next section begins in measure 36 with a bass line derived from the opening motive through melodic inversion (a line remarkably similar to the combined bass/treble line in the A-Major *Two*-Part Invention, Number Twelve, at measures 7-8 and 16-17). It is taken through five, one-bar sequential stages (36-41) rising by fourth, with corresponding chordal root movement (D, G, C, F, Bb) which accommodates modulations upward by seventh (downward by second) approximately every other measure, from D minor to C minor to Bb major. The soprano, presenting alto material from measures 2-3, is also sequential, but with *two*-bar stages (37-38/39-40), partially doubled at the lower third by the alto, which creates, along with the soprano, a double suspension across the bar-line into measure 40 (as opposed to a single suspension, which occurs in the soprano two measures earlier). The soprano's second stage lies down one degree from its first and thus ties in with the upper-seventh transposition provided by *two*, one-measure sequential statements at the upper fourth in the bass.

Example 11-5.  Measures 36-41

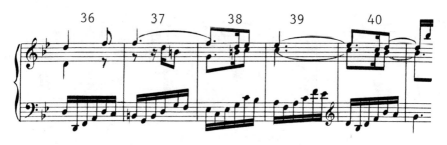

At measures 41-43, the alto proceeds with a series of rising melodic fourths, each of which falls by fifth to create more sequence by descending second. The upper notes of these fourths, because of the agogic stress that carries them across the bar-line--become dissonant with the bass each time the bass changes, at the beginning of the measure. The soprano, here, takes up a four-note version of the original motive with interval contraction which turns what originally was an ascending octave into an ascending sixth, the top note of which is also stressed agogically across the bar-line. The key reverts to G minor at about the point where the alto, having concluded its rising fourths, starts a new sequence based upon the original motive's initial fragment in melodic inversion, creating momentarily another doubled leading tone (measure 44).

A Neapolitan sixth chord lends color to the harmony at the end of measure 45, as the upper voices' material starts becoming less derivative in preparation for an upcoming cadence at 47-48; the bass, however, keeps alive the dotted-note rhythmic pattern which has persisted intermittently since the time it was introduced by the alto in measure 3, first in association with pitches which invert those of the alto line from 3 (measure 46), then more freely.

Example 11-6.  Measures 41-48

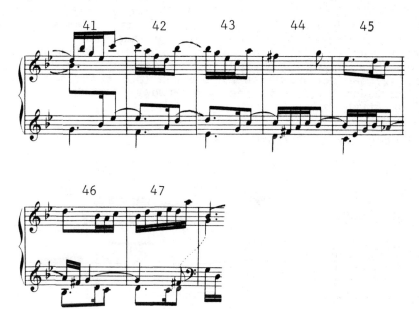

The passage at measures 48-51 brings back an earlier passage from 17-20 (which, in turn, is at least partially based upon the still earlier one beginning at 11), the alto line from before now being situated down an octave in the bass (except where it momentarily parts company in measure 50), and the bass line from before being situated in the alto at both the upper octave and the unison because of every-other-measure octave displacement, so that invertible counterpoint occurs between these lower two voices beneath the same top line, down an octave. The use of Ab by the soprano during measure 51 (in lieu of Bb by the same voice during measure 20) reflects different tonal conditions between the endings of these two otherwise very similar passages.

During the course of this latter passage and after-
wards, the soprano exploits one sequence after another.
Overlapping the one which starts at measure 48 is another which starts on the second sixteenth note of 49,
and this one, having two, two-bar stages that fall by
second, is followed by another, having two *one*-bar stages that also fall by second, starting on the second sixteenth of 53, then another, with stages that rise by
third, starting on the second sixteenth of 55. Still another soprano sequence unfolds then during measures 57-
58.  The lower two voices, meanwhile, having completed
their own sequences or sequence-like lines during measures 48-52, move in tenths with each other (53-55),
after which the alto falls silent as the bass brings
back the pervasive dotted-note rhythmic pattern, first
with the alto's melodic configuration from measure 3
(at 55), then freely, prior to establishing a dominant
pedal, the second measure of which (58) recalls an earlier measure (24) in the lower two voices down a perfect fifth.

Example 11-7.  Measures 48-59

Measures 59-62 bring about a return of the passage from 25-28, also down a perfect fifth (from D minor to G minor), after which the bass continues to sustain its pedal, as dominant harmony is arpeggiated all the way to the ninth by the upper voices.

Example 11-8.   Measures 59-65

A late return of the first six measures of the sinfonia--verbatim in all three voice-parts after the soprano's initial Eb--ensues at 65-70.  The bass and alto at 71, the penultimate measure, are strict with themselves from 7, but in conjunction with the soprano, they also bring back material from 15 transposed down a third (from the relative major key to the tonic) during this measure, and as things turn out, the sinfonia, itself, ends with a transposed restatement of the first principal section's ending, a condition which, to some extent, characterizes the F-Minor Sinfonia (Number Nine).

Example 11-9.   Measures 65-72

CHAPTER 12: SINFONIA NUMBER TWELVE (A MAJOR)


Like the D-Major Sinfonia (Number Three), the A-Major Sinfonia has a subject in the soprano which can be construed either as a non-modulating idea (ending on beat three of measure 2) followed by a half-bar link, or as a longer, modulating idea (ending on beat one of measure 3) *not* followed by a link, but since six of the seven subject or answer statements found throughout the course of this piece make use of the appendage in question (from the last half of measure 2)--or its inversion--it seems most logical for one to consider it an intrinsic part of the subject, itself, a part which carries the subject into the dominant key and thus precludes the employment of a real answer.

By this interpretation, the subject has three distinct parts: motive one (a head motive) starting directly on the first beat and ending with an agogically stressed A in measure 1; motive two (a middle motive) beginning with the changing-tone configuration during the final beat of measure 1 and continuing with a broken pedal which creates a compound melody through the first half of measure 2; and motive three (a tail motive), which modulates its way into measure 3. Beneath this subject, an eighth-note line made initially staccato in nature by rests which intervene between notes, is situated in the bass. Portions of this line subjected to various modifications reappear periodically with the subject or answer in the manner of a countersubject (Example 12-1).

The soprano is answered (imitated) by the alto at the dominant (specifically the lower fourth) during measure 3 and the first part of 4, after which instead of taking the usual path of response to a modulating subject, with imitation at the subdominant (lower fifth) for its closing portion, the alto simply inverts motive three, starting it on G♯ and ending it on C♯, a fifth

101

Example 12-1.   Measures 1-3

below, in response to the subject's motive three, which
starts on C♯ and ends on G♯, a fifth *above*. This procedure ingeniously sidesteps the problem of where to
make the initial tonal adjustment (a problem of some
magnitude with this particular idea), since the upside-
down tail motive occupies the same amount of space as
the right-side-up tail motive but in the opposite direction, and the modulation back to the tonic key--up
a fourth or down a fifth in response to the tonal movement up a fifth or down a fourth within the subject--is
still gracefully accomplished. This somewhat unusual
tonal answer is accompanied in the bass by transposed
countersubject material (exhibiting octave displacement
downward for its initial note and upward for its final
note), and in the soprano by a rhythmically altered account of the subject's tail motive upside-down, followed by freer, less derivative syncopated material,
then a varied, *un*inverted statement of a portion of the
tail.

Example 12-2.   Measures 3-5

There is no modulatory need for a link between the
second and third entries in contrapuntal pieces such as
this one which exploit a modulating subject and answer,
and, in fact, none is used here. The third entry (mea-

sures 4-6, in the bass) begins at the lower octave with the first entry and remains strict until the first note of measure 7, which varies the procedure from before by setting off the second half-bar stage of a sequence that unites with the preceding half-bar closing portion of the subject as a first stage and provides a brief link (beats one and two of measure 7) leading to another statement of the tonal answer by the soprano. Along with this bass entry, the upper voices have partially derivative and partially free material, the former concentrated mostly in measure 5, which exhibits a slightly ornamented, dotted-note account of the countersubject's first three beats in sequence by the soprano, above a more heavily ornamented account (likewise in sequence) at the lower third by the alto, these two lines creating a chain of suspensions (which includes the less usual six/five-four suspension) over the bass.

The additional soprano entry that gets under way with the tied E in measure 7 functions as a redundant entry, since--within the framework of this opening exposition--it duplicates the alto's tonal answer from measures 3-5 at the upper octave, in a voice-part, which has already presented the subject. Bits and pieces from before are found in the alto, which has a transposed version of a fragment from the answer's tail motive followed by a syncopated thought (found earlier during the first part of measure 6 as well as several times later), at measure 8, and in the bass, which *begins* a third stage to the sequence from before, during the last half of measure 7, but never completes it.

Example 12-3.  Measures 5-9

An episode of about five-and-one-half measures gets
under way in the middle of measure 9 with immediate
chromatic movement in the direction of F# minor, followed by fluctuating tonalities prior to the time it
concludes, back in F# minor, with an imperfect authentic cadence at measures 14-15. Motive one from the subject in two slightly different forms--each minus the
first note and each with a lengthened final note--is
ubiquitous throughout most of this episode in the upper
voices, in counterpoint, during the first few measures,
with various modified presentations of motive two from
the subject in the bass.

The alto version of motive one is the original one,
and it appears sequentially with the better part of
four, four-beat stages which descend by second starting
in the middle of measure 9. The soprano imitates the
alto somewhat canonically, but its failure to change
direction into the sustained half-note each time pre-
vents the canon from being strict, although within its
own frame of reference, the soprano is sequential like
the alto. So too is the bass with its reshaped asser-
tion of motive two, still exploiting a compound melody,
but with a pedal broken by pitches that create smaller
intervals than before.

The sequence breaks during measure 13, where the
soprano takes up what the alto has just had (motive one

in its original form--minus the first note) and treats it in a sequential manner with stages now just half as long as the preceding ones, because the final note of each one has been shortened. As the bass sustains a C♯ pedal, the alto doubles the first stage of the soprano's sequence at the lower third before becoming free. A cross relation occurs between D♯ in the soprano and D-natural in the bass within measure 14, as this passage sorts out differences between C♯ minor and F♯ minor in favor of the latter, the relative minor key, in time for the conclusion of section one.

Example 12-4. Measures 9-15

An even more striking chromatic circumstance results from a double inflection between E♯ in the bass and
E-natural in the soprano during measure 15, where the
bass launches a new section with a statement of the answer, embellished by a single note (B) immediately pri-
or to its upside-down motive three, in measure 16. No
other entry--subject or answer--appears in the vicinity
of this isolated entry, which, from the middle of measure 15 to the middle of 16, is accompanied by the soprano, and to some extent the alto, with a portion of
the material found during the earlier bass presentation
of the subject, from the middle of 5 to the middle of
6. In fact, the continuation of this passage at 17 is
very much like the continuation at 7, since there is a
sequential outgrowth of the tail motive in both instances, but the subject's *uninverted* tail motive was
used previously, with a sequence falling by degree, and
the answer's *inverted* tail motive is used here, with a
sequence *rising* by degree. Furthermore, there are four
complete half-bar stages to this sequence, and fewer
than three, to the earlier one, which is broken in upon
by the redundant entry. So the tail motive is generating an episode here, as opposed to a brief link before, and at least part of the bass's sequential activity is matched by similar activity in the upper two
voices, using material similar to that used from the
middle of 6 to the middle of 7.

The key of A major returns as the answer is ending
and the episode beginning, and it remains for the rest
of the sinfonia, although there are tonicizations such
as that which occurs within the first half of measure
18, where a dominant seventh chord of the dominant sets
up a dominant pedal point, over which a suspension with
a highly deferred resolution is initially situated.

Example 12-5.   Measures 15-19

The beginning of this pedal, which is sustained for approximately six beats, marks the conclusion of isolated sequential treatment of the third motive from the answer and the beginning of less extensive isolated sequential treatment of its first motive, still without the first note, as in the previous episode. In fact, the entire six-beat passage which starts at measure 13 and continues through the first half of measure 14 reappears in transposition to A major and with the upper pair of voices exchanged in invertible counterpoint at the octave here (from the middle of measure 18 to the end of 19). Tonicization of the dominant results from the use of D♯ several times within measure 19, creating a certain amount of clash with the dominant pedal.

The soprano's sixteenth notes found at the beginning of measure 20 derive from the answer's tail motive shifted by a half-beat. The bass, after having temporarily doubled the soprano at the lower tenth (plus an octave), takes up a version of motive two which is like that used starting in the middle of measure 9, but with octave displacement between the moving (non-pedal) portion of the compound melody, which is transposed down a third from before, and the broken pedal, itself, which is transposed up a sixth, so that the moving portion of the compound melody is situated *below* the broken pedal, rather than above. The same approach to sequence that was taken by the bass before is taken here in a slightly abbreviated manner, with three one-bar stages appearing from the middle of 20 to the middle of 23 before the pattern breaks. The upper two voices likewise bring back their material from the earlier passage, but starting a half measure later than before in relationship to the bass, and exploiting invertible counterpoint at the octave (measures 21-22-23/10-11-12) with each other (Example 12-6).

Measure 24 brings about a reappearance of the one-

Example 12-6.  Measures 18-24

and-one-half-measure passage starting at measure 5, with
the bass down an octave and the upper two voices situated in invertible counterpoint with each other.  An
element of return is brought about by the reintroduc-
tion of the subject in the tonic key, even though it
relates back to the third entry of the piece rather
than the first, and even though the statement is in-
complete--the only statement of the piece to omit motive three, which is here supplanted by most of the
syncopated thought from just before in the soprano (and
earlier in the alto, at measures 6, 8-9, and 16).  The
soprano, which breaks in upon the bass prematurely, with
imitation at the double octave, does go ahead and virtually complete the subject by including this tail motive, but with D-natural rather than D♯, thus avoiding
a modulation into the dominant key, and with the final

note omitted to allow for a sequential continuation of motive three like the one at measure 7. In fact, the *last* half of 27 brings back the *first* half of 7 with the bass line up an octave here in the soprano, the soprano line down an octave in the alto, and the alto line down an octave in the bass, all of which results in invertible counterpoint involving two pairs of melodic lines. Sequence is carried one stage further during this latter passage.

Example 12-7.  Measures 24-28

This isolated sequential treatment based upon motive three and its contrapuntal adjuncts is followed by similar treatment involving motive one (still without its first note), which has been allotted four half-bar stages falling by second (from the middle of 28 to the middle of 32) in the alto, as the bass sustains a dominant pedal and the soprano gets caught up in sequence too, but on less derivative material, with two different half-bar ideas, each of which has two stages, the first such sequence involving movement upward by fourth, and the second, movement downward by second. The dominant chord is briefly tonicized within the last beat of measure 30, after which a cadential six-four chord (with a double escape tone) and a dominant chord (with an anticipation) set up the conclusion.

Example 12-8.   Measures 28-31

# CHAPTER 13: SINFONIA NUMBER THIRTEEN (A MINOR)

The A-Minor Sinfonia's opening exposition--like much of the rest of the piece--unfolds in even, four-measure units (resulting from cadences or cadence-like progressions located at measures 3-4, 7-8, 11-12, and 15-16) which produce an effect somewhat like that of antecedent and consequent phrases, as in homophonic music. The soprano's sixteenth-note motion in measure 4 (much like the motion that often provides "follow-through" in the final measure of a non-concluding homophonic phrase) complicates the issue of exactly where the subject ends, an issue further clouded by the location of the pivot chord in a modulation from the tonic key to the dominant key *prior* to the time the answer begins (within measure 4) rather than just *as*, or after it begins--the usual procedure, except, of course, with a modulating subject; this subject, however (the only generating idea among all the generating ideas of the *Sinfonias* to avoid disjunct motion entirely), has not been treated like a modulating subject, because it has not been answered tonally.

The eighth-note portion of the bass idea underlying the subject during the first few measures is found, transposed into E minor with its initial two notes rearranged at the octave, beneath a real answer in the alto during measure 5 and after, but this constitutes the only other appearance of the idea, so it is not much of a countersubject; nor is the soprano material of the same passage, an outgrowth of the subject's fourth measure, found during measures 13-16 in the alto (transposed, and without the soprano's anticipation from the end of 7), but nowhere else, completely intact (Example 13-1).

This soprano line does, however, instigate a link (measures 9-12), which almost immediately introduces Bb, forcing a key change from E minor back to A minor *through*

111

Example 13-1.   Measures 1-9

D minor (a closely related key) rather than B minor (a non closely related key), which might otherwise have resulted. The ornamentation of a highly ornamented four-three suspension gets this link under way in the soprano above a sustained D in the alto, which now and throughout this link, occupies the lowest position in a two-voice texture, since the bass has dropped out. The alto in measure 10 freely switches roles with the soprano from 9, as the passage pivots back to A minor, after which the two voices re-exchange (11) before joining forces in sixths to conclude the link, which is characterized throughout by sixteenth notes having a falling contour.

The bass entry which closes out the opening exposition at measures 13-16 is the last one having all four bars intact without any modifying features. In addition to the soprano material of measures 5-8, which shows up here in the alto at the lower perfect twelfth (slightly skeletonized in measure 15), this entry is accompanied in the soprano by an inversion of the pattern from 5 (in 15), among other things (Example 13-2).

The fourth bar of this bass entry (16)--which is strict with the opening entry's fourth bar at the lower double octave, and the subsequent alto entry's at the

Example 13-2. Measures 9-17

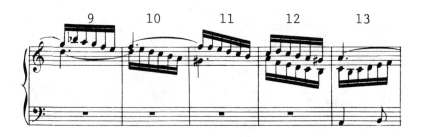

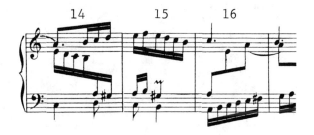

lower perfect twelfth--produces tonal movement *not* upward by fifth (as with the soprano entry at measure 4)
nor downward by second (as with the alto entry at 8),
but rather upward by third, from A minor to C major.
The versatility of the tonic chord as a pivot chord,
becoming respectively the subdominant (measure 4), supertonic (measure 8), and submediant (measure 16), in
the new key is thus vividly shown, as is the fact that
the melodic material which defines this chord has no
inevitable inclination in any one particular tonal direction.

Sixteenth notes which are mostly ascending, in contrast to those of the link beginning in measure 9 which
are mostly descending, provide the chief thematic material of the episode that begins in measure 17 and concludes the first section of the sinfonia at the beginning of 21 in the relative major key. These sixteenths
relate to and continue the bass line of measure 16 up
to the octave and beyond before they are acquired by
the soprano and alto, which have them doubled in thirds
(18), then tenths (19). The soprano alone retains sixteenths, now mostly in a descending fashion, into the
end of the section (Example 13-3).

The second section, set off from the first more by

Example 13-3.   Measures 17-21

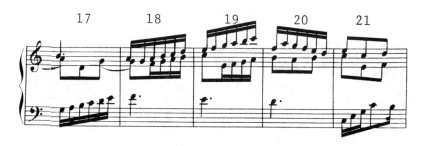

new treatment of old material than by a substantive cadence, begins with a C-major statement of the subject
by the soprano, which has a slightly deferred, abbreviated first note and a transposition of the bulk of its
sixteenth-note afterthought at the lower fifth from where
it would lie if it followed the plan used by all entries within the first section. The alto doubles all
of this soprano line down a sixth, except for the transposed sixteenth-note segment. The bass accompanies these
events with a line, much of which is to become the most
pervasive countersubject of the piece. This line is
largely characterized by arpeggiated triadic movement,
initially in the manner of a palindrome, back and forth
between small C (c) and middle C (c'), with the bass
suspension resulting from the use of syncopation. Both
embellishment (measure 23) and skeletonization (24) occur with this bass line in relationship to its first
measure (21).

During most of the next four measures (25-28), the
alto provides its own C-major statement of the subject
by imitating the soprano from 21 and after at the unison while the soprano imitates the alto at the upper
octave, so invertible counterpoint is displayed between
the upper voices of these two four-bar passages. Material from the first measure of the bass's countersubject (21) shows up with the *second* measure of this alto
entry (26) up an octave in the bass, but the rest of
this countersubject has not been included. The alto
rounds off its subject statement at measure 28 by employing sixteenth notes in free melodic inversion with
those from the original, section-one statements (Example 13-4).

What amounts to virtually the second eight-measure
stage of a sixteen-measure sequence (starting at 21)
unfolds in the soprano from 29 *into* but not through 36,

Example 13-4.  Measures 21-29

with transposition up a second from C major to D minor.
The alto material of its first four measures (29-32) is
relatively free, but during the following measures (33
and after), the alto, like the soprano, simply brings
back what it, itself, has at 25-27 transposed from C major to D minor. The bass initially exploits melodic in-
version--with the soprano line from 24, here at 29, and
with the soprano line from 5, here at 30 and 32 (like
the soprano at 15)--after which it returns *its* own line,
*not* from 25-27, but rather 21-23 (the new countersubject), with the same upward-by-second transposition.

Example 13-5.  Measures 29-36

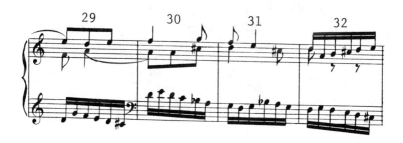

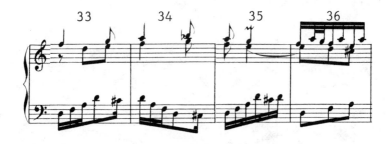

Measure 36 brings the alto's subject statement to a close in a decidedly different manner from before, with all eighth notes, and at the same time introduces in the soprano new material which--because of its use of thirty-second notes--is the most active material in the sinfonia. This material inaugurates an episode in which all three voices are sequential with two, two-bar stages, each stage starting at a slightly different location in measure 36: the soprano's within beat one, the alto's on beat two, and the bass's (which is free) on beat three. A change in tonality from D minor back to C major is reflected by the appearance of each voice part's second stage down one scale degree from the first, although octave displacement in the bass, starting with the second note of its second stage (C, at the beginning of measure 39), results in transposition up a seventh rather than down a second. A modulation on to G major (the subtonic major key) takes place near the end of the episode.

Example 13-6.  Measures 36-41

Another version of the subject appears in the bass, now in G major, starting in measure 41 and (like the alto in 36) manifesting eighth-note motion within its fourth measure (44). About half of the bass counter-subject from 21 and after is situated in the soprano, creating invertible counterpoint between the first half of this passage and the corresponding part of the ear-lier passage, as the alto momentarily rests and then begins imitating the bass line at the upper octave in stretto, with a one-bar time interval (42-43-44), prior to continuing with imitation of most of the *soprano* line from 43, at the lower perfect fifth and with a *two*-bar time interval, as a brief, four-measure episode is set off.

The alto, in fact, continues imitating the soprano at the lower fifth for another four beats, as the so-prano--all in even eighth-notes--provides a short se-quence (45-46), and the bass presents the first two bars of the subject, inverted, in C major. The *bass* then (47-49) takes up the previous soprano line from 43-45 (which has just been imitated by the alto at 45-47), in transposition (with octave displacement between the in-itial two notes of 48), and the alto (47) furnishes the *un*inverted third bar of the subject on the scale de-grees for C major, as a modulation which restores A mi-nor, the tonic key, is taking place. This is followed in the alto by a simulation of the same third bar of the subject (48), now on scale degrees appropriate to A minor. The cadence at 48-49 is only moderately con-clusive in nature, despite the suggestion of hemiola and other strong cadential tendencies of the syncopated soprano line which precedes it (Example 13-7).

A final system of subject entries--one for each voice-part at a different octave level--is launched at measure 49 by the alto, which starts a beat late (like most of the voices presenting subjects since the start of section two) and ends with sixteenth notes shaped

Example 13-7.   Measures 41-49

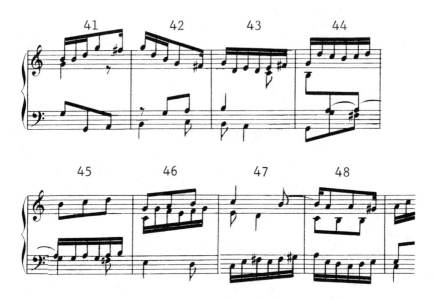

somewhat like those in the soprano at 24 and 32.   Countersubject material from the bass at 21-22-23 shows up
here in the soprano (49-50-51), creating more invertible counterpoint, and the upside-down subject's beginning part found earlier in the bass at 45-46 comes back
here (still in the bass) as an accompaniment to the
*ending* of the *un*inverted alto entry (51-52).

The alto is then imitated at the lower octave by
the bass (at 53 and after), starting directly on beat
one again and doubled by the soprano at the upper tenth
plus an octave, enclosing the countersubject in the alto.   The association of these three contrapuntal lines,
first at 21-23, then 33-35, and now 53-55, constitutes
an incipient form of triple counterpoint, which real-
izes half of the total number of possibilities for inversion (three out of six), but the countersubject is
never inverted with the line that doubles the subject.

Measure 56 generates an episode much like the one
back at 36 and after because of its employment of the
same rhythmically active material; however, sequence on
this material now has one-measure stages (in the alto
at 56-58 and soprano at 58-60) rather than two-measure
stages as before, and imitation, conversely, now has a
two-bar--not a one-bar--time interval (producing invertible counterpoint at the tenth in the same two voices).

As a final statement of the subject is brought in by the soprano starting in measure 60, this episodic material continues as accompaniment, showing up in its strict form starting on E (in the alto at 60, the bass at 61, and the alto again at 63--all in different octaves) as well as a freer form on B (in the bass at 62). The final statement of this material, which originated in measure 36, appears in conjunction with a double suspension (dissonant on the first beat of 63) having both resolutions--the lower one ornamented--displaced by an octave (up a seventh rather than down a second), and it concludes the piece with a perfect authentic cadence--the only such cadence found in this sinfonia. A Picardy third is present in the last chord.

Example 13-8. Measures 49-64

# CHAPTER 14: SINFONIA NUMBER FOURTEEN (Bb MAJOR)

The subject upon which this piece is based has descending, filled-in, tonic-to-dominant melodic movement
in the alto, which is responded to tonally during the
answer (beginning in the soprano slightly late--on the
second half of beat one in measure 2) with descending,
filled-in dominant-to-tonic movement. The repeated note
following the tie in the subject is therefore supplanted
by a note that descends conjunctly in the answer, changing the interval of imitation from the upper fifth for
the first note of the answer to the upper fourth for
the subsequent four-note fragment, after which the rising third (to D) causes a reversion to imitation at the
fifth.

Both subject and answer exhibit an overall contour
that drops from one octave level to another, the subject embracing the tonic (Bb), and the answer, the dominant (F). E-natural, however, is not introduced until
just prior to the fourth beat of measure 2, where it
conveys nothing more than a passing tonicization of the
dominant triad (which, itself, does not appear as the
immediate chord of resolution), so the answer is situated *at* the dominant in Bb major rather than *in* the key
of F major. Neither the eighth-note line of measure 1
in the bass nor the quarter-note line of measure 2 is
particularly recurrent; the alto's first beat of measure 2, on the other hand, does encompass a triadic configuration which receives some attention intermittently
throughout the piece, and the material of its second
beat additionally relates to that of the answer's third
beat (Example 14-1).

During the link which unfolds in measure three,
the soprano employs a freely sequential pattern that
capitalizes upon disjunct motion in falling sixteenth
notes followed by rising eighth notes, and the bass imitates the soprano in stretto at the lower tenth with a

121

Example 14-1.   Measures 1-3

one-beat time interval. The slower-moving alto voice
employs material (like the eighth-note material in the
soprano) from the answer's third beat in various transpositions, and its ending prepares a suspension which
is ornamented in such a fashion within the first beat
of measure 4 as to reproduce a brief fragment from the
corresponding location in measure 2 at the upper octave, along with the beginning of a bass statement of
the subject which rounds out the opening exposition at
the lower octave with the original soprano statement.

Example 14-2.   Measures 3-5

    The last five notes of this bass entry form the
first stage of a sequence, the second and third stages
of which come at the successively lower third during
measure 5 and the very beginning of 6.  The alto is sequential along with the bass (creating consecutive perfect fifths within beats one and three), while the soprano descends in a conjunct, syncopated manner. During
measure 6, the soprano resumes a more rhythmically active
role by bringing back a modified account of its material
from the link as well as alto material from the first half
of 2 (and 4), and again--as in measure 3--the bass imitates the soprano in stretto after one beat, first at the
lower fifth (and twelfth, because of octave displacement),
and then at the lower eleventh (Example 14-3).

    An altered alto entry of the subject--situated on

Example 14-3. Measures 4-7

the same lines and spaces of the staff as the opening
alto subject but with certain notes inflected--starts
at measure 7 in Bb major (which has persisted throughout the opening exposition and subsequent episode up to
this point, having been tempered only by brief tonicizations of the dominant and subdominant chords) and modulates through G minor into C minor, ending there on the
third of the dominant seventh chord at the beginning of
measure 8. This entry, therefore, from start to finish,
encompasses a diminished octave (Bb to B-natural) rather than a perfect octave.

By way of response, the soprano brings in what might
be termed a *hybrid* entry, one which is initially shaped
like the subject--although it starts a half beat late,
on the fifth degree, like the answer--then the answer's
rising third, and *then* a descending tritone, which involves expansion above and beyond the intervalic size of
both subject and answer at this point. Its imitation of
the preceding alto line at the sixth, however, remains
constant except for one note (the eighth note, F).

As subordinate material to this pair of entries,
the soprano in measure 7 recalls a portion of its syncopated line from measures 4-5, and the bass presents
the subject's opening sixteenth-note fragment sequentially, with one-beat stages, during the last part of
7 and first part of 8. Last-minute doubling by the alto of the soprano entry's conclusion at the end of 8 is
also noteworthy. The bass's sixteenth-note fragment,
then, after having briefly lapsed, is temporarily re-
vived (still in a sequential fashion) at the end of 8
and beginning of 9, fragmentarily anticipating alto material that imitates a substantial portion (all but the
first and last notes) of the hybrid entry located in
the soprano a measure before, down a sixth. The concluding fifth is now replaced by a tied note that functions as the fourth of a four-three suspension on the
first beat of measure 10, softening the effect of ca-

dence implicit in the dominant-seventh-to-tonic harmonic progression, and contributing to a deferral of the
section's end by a couple of measures.

A Picardy-third effect promoted by the E-natural
resolution of this suspension fuels a change of key into F major, in which key the bass then presents a tonal answer which is strict with the original answer except for transposition and the size of its closing interval (a falling seventh instead of a falling fifth).
The initial portion of this answer is imitated in stretto by the alto at the seventh and a one-beat time interval. Descending arpeggiated triads in sixteenth-note
groupings like those found earlier during measures 3
and 6 provide the chief derivative material of measure
11, in the alto and bass, after which a perfect authentic cadence (complete with an anticipation on the dominant chord) brings the first principal section of the
sinfonia to a close in the dominant major key.

Example 14-4.  Measures 7-12

The second section gets under way with a soprano statement of the hybrid entry up a second from where it was originally situated at measures 8-9 (in D minor--at least for its closing portion--instead of C minor, as before), and the alto imitates the soprano a beat later in stretto, exploiting a metrically displaced account of the generating idea which is closer to the answer than to the subject, although not completely strict as either. This stretto begins at the lower seventh, but because of its answer-like beginning (without the re-peated note) as opposed to the soprano's *subject*-like beginning (*with* the repeated note), it switches to the lower octave almost immediately and remains intact at this interval until its conclusion on the second beat of measure 13. The subject's beginning sixteenth-note fragment, having been touched upon by the bass during the opening portion of both measure 12 and measure 13, dominates the scene in all voices, mostly upside-down, from the middle of measure 13 to the middle of 14, at which point the third perfect authentic harmonic pro-gression within the space of five measures takes place--this one in D minor.

Example 14-5. Measures 12-14

More stretto is featured at the middle of 14, where the soprano sets off a fairly long chain of back-to-back entries by coming out with a modified tonal answer which modulates very quickly into C minor, making use of intervals which--like those of certain previous entries--have been adjusted in terms of both numerical size and quality, the most noticeable of which perhaps is the augmented fifth from B-natural down to Eb in measure 15. The alto is mostly silent here, but the bass imitates about half of this soprano entry--including its one-note prefix (D)--in stretto at the lower octave with a one-beat time interval, after which the alto resumes (right on the heels of the soprano entry's conclusion) by providing imitation at the lower fourth, starting (in measure 15) on C, thus suggesting a continuation in F major, since this entry (as well as the one that precedes it) is initially shaped like the tonal answer rather than the subject; however, a modulation from C minor into Bb major, and from there, on into Eb major (as a consequence of the bass's employment of Ab along with the ending note) causes it (like all the entries that precede it within section two) to occupy scale degrees other than those of the original subject and answer in terms of the prevailing tonal center.

This change into Eb major sets off another type of hybrid entry, one starting like the tonal answer (without a repeated note) on the second scale degree (F, at the end of measure 16) in the alto and migrating in *durchbrochene-Arbeit* fashion almost immediately to the bass, where all the rest of the entry unfolds, down an octave (doubled in sixths by the soprano for a short time) exactly like the subject, *on* the original scale degrees within the context of Eb major.

The subsequent entry, coming in just as this one is concluding, is essentially a tonal answer which begins on G in the soprano and utilizes interval expansion within beat one of measure 18 (from C up to F) and also from beat one to beat two (F down to Bb). It modulates quickly into Bb major, the tonic key, which is now returning for the final time, unfolding on scale degrees which do *not* conform to the original scheme. A highly modified entry in the alto beginning on C (beat four of measure 17) creates some effect of stretto in conjunction with this soprano statement, and before this alto entry has concluded, the soprano starts sequencing itself at the lower third, completing its second stage during measure 19, where a third stage *begins*, but does not follow through. The second stage of the soprano sequence, meanwhile, is imitated in stretto somewhat more strictly this time by the alto, which has an exact account of the original tonal answer from measures 2-3 at the lower octave, except for metrical displacement which causes the entry to start and finish on weak beats rather than strong; most of the way through this entry at 18-19, therefore, the alto imitates the soprano at the lower seventh. After having completed *its* entry back in 17, the bass becomes momentarily syncopated, then starts dealing with sixteenth-note fragments taken from the subject's opening once again and treated sequentially during the latter portions of 18 and 19.

Example 14-6. Measures 14-20

The principal impression of return is achieved at measures 20-22, where the subject is reintroduced by the alto in the tonic key, with interval expansion that produces A instead of G on the last half of the third beat in measure 20, a change which harmonically accommodates the tonal answer--presented by the soprano in duplication of the voicing from the beginning of the piece--in a looser stretto than was exhibited in previous stretto passages, with a two-beat (rather than a one-beat) time interval. The soprano, which conveys the answer strictly, except for syncopation that causes a

slightly deferred final note, is, in turn, imitated in
stretto by the bass at the same (two-beat) time interval (producing a very brief moment of invertible counterpoint), but with the final note (the first bass note
of measure 22) changed. So the return involves a compressed version of the opening, with a subject-answer-
answer arrangement employing stretto, as opposed to a
subject-answer-subject arrangement without stretto.

As the bass is finishing its tonal answer, the soprano (beats three and four of measure 21) brings back
the alto fragment from the first half of measure 2, up
an octave, setting off a brief coda-like passage during
the last three measures of the sinfonia. This passage
has no complete entries of the subject or answer, and,
in fact, only free motivic relationships with earlier
material. Two half-bar sequential stages are found in
each of the three voice-parts during measure 22 (where
tonicization of the subdominant lends a closing quality
to the passage), after which both material *and* treatment become free. The bass at the beginning of 23 is
noteworthy for its treatment of the suspension--one of
several, mostly ornamented, suspensions employed during
the last few measures (including a double suspension on
beat three of measure 21)--because its dissonance, having been stated, is displaced upward by an octave before being resolved on the second beat. Thirty-second
notes are introduced as part of a descending Bb-major
scale in the soprano and continued partly past the octave by the alto, lending a sudden burst of rhythmic
activity to the beats which precede the final cadence
chords.

Example 14-7. Measures 20-24

# CHAPTER 15:  SINFONIA NUMBER FIFTEEN (B MINOR)

This piece opens more like a *two*-part invention than a sinfonia (*three*-part invention), for like Sinfonia Number Two in C Minor which is also atypical, it employs opening imitation at the lower *octave*, rather than the lower fourth or upper fifth, *not*, however, in the alto as in Number Two--and, in fact, all the other sinfonias which start with subjects or motives in the soprano--but rather in the bass (as in the *Two-Part Inventions*). Prior to this imitation. the bass accompanies the soprano with a countersubject, which after having supported the subject's even sixteenth notes (in nine/sixteen meter, the only such use of this meter in Bach's inventions and sinfonias) with tonic harmony in measure 1 and dominant harmony in measure 2, resolves and then falls silent as the subject arpeggiates the the tonic triad through different positions, entirely in thirty-second notes, leaving a somewhat unusual monophonic texture throughout most of measure 3.

The bass takes over the subject an octave lower, as the soprano takes over the countersubject an octave higher at measure 4 (creating invertible counterpoint at the double octave), and during the subject's third measure (6), the soprano does service above and beyond what the bass does in measure 3, by arpeggiating the B-minor triad on a note-against-note basis with the bass, adhering to the same contour within the framework of its different location in the scale (Example 15-1).

The alto completes the opening exposition's voicing scheme by presenting, during measure 7, a false (incomplete) entry involving the first nine notes of the subject exactly as they are found at the beginning. This false entry generates a sequential episode given over initially to back-and-forth imitative statements which create invertible counterpoint from one bar to

131

Example 15-1.   Measures 1-7

the next between the upper two voices, for the alto is--
from its second note of measure 7--imitated at the upper fourth by the soprano, and the soprano at the lower
fifth by the alto, during measure 8.  These two measures, which point away from B minor down one degree in
the direction of A major, together form the first stage
of a sequence, the second stage of which follows during
9-10, likewise down one degree.

The bass, meanwhile, employing material from the
countersubject's first measure, verbatim, has a rising
fourth (in lieu of the original falling second) attached
across the bar-line in such a way that a one-bar unit
is created from the second beat of measure 7 to the
second beat of 8, and this unit--just half as long as
the overlying unit in the upper voices--is also sequenced, but at the lower fifth, with four stages rather than two, the third and fourth stages compositely

being situated a ninth down from the first and second, and thus causing sequential treatment which jibes (an octave further away) with that of the upper voices.

Example 15-2.  Measures 7-11

More sequence unfolds during the latter portion of this episode at 11-13, where the key shifts to D major, as the alto mostly rests, and the outer voices focus on thirty-second-note material from the second beat of the subject's third measure. In measure 11, which contains the new sequence's first stage, this material is presented by the soprano on beat one and imitated by the bass at the lower tenth on beat two, after which these two voices join forces in compound tenths on beat three (the bass, with a second one-*beat* sequential stage). Measure 12 then sequences 11 down one degree in both voices, and 13 provides a third one-bar stage down another degree in the bass. About midway through this three-bar passage (starting on the third beat of measure 12), the bass's employment of the treble's five-*beat* unit from the beginning of the passage at the lower double octave--along with the treble's employment of the bass's two-beat sequence from the second and third beats of measure 11 at the upper single octave during the first two beats of measure 13, where invertible counterpoint is therefore momentarily created--renews, during the passage's second portion, the essential harmonic plan of its first portion, with emphasis on root movement by descending third from one chord to the next (subdominant, supertonic, dominant, mediant, and ton-ic). Because of the emphasis on this type of root move-ment, section one is brought to a rather weak conclu-sion, in D major.

Example 15-3.   Measures 11-14

A new section is defined at measure 14 mostly by the reappearance of the subject in the relative major key following the preceding episode. The alto, re-en-tering after a rest of almost three measures, is now given its first opportunity to present the entire sub-ject (just as the bass voice is given the same opportu-nity at the corresponding location in the C-Minor Sin-fonia), as the soprano drops out, reinstating the two-voice texture which has prevailed throughout most of this piece so far, almost immediately.

This alto entry, however, is not completely strict with the subject entries at the beginning of the sin-fonia, for aside from having been placed into a new key with a different mode, it has been given a last mea-sure (16) which--starting with the last thirty-second note of the first compound beat (B)--changes the inter-val of transposition, from the lower sixth with the o-pening entry to the lower fifth, through the process of interval contraction, directing the passage tonally from D major up a fifth to A major, on different scale degrees within the key. Had this entry been situated at the beginning of the sinfonia, traditional imitative

procedures would have called for a tonal answer by way
of response, but here during section two the soprano
imitates at the perfect fifth all the way over to the
entry's final note, the first note of measure 20 (which
is free, being neither tonal nor real), and because of
this, the soprano entry too modulates up a fifth, from
A major to E minor.

Material from the countersubject's first measure
is employed by the bass to accompany the alto statement's first *and* second measures (14 and 15), whereas
material from the countersubject's *second* measure is
employed to accompany the alto statement's *third* measure (16). During the ensuing soprano statement, the
bass becomes less active, but the *alto* now provides material from the countersubject's first measure along
with the first measure of the statement (17) and from
its second measure along with both the second *and* third
measures (18 and 19) in a sequential fashion.

Example 15-4.   Measures 14-20

The passage at 20-23 (and after), which modulates quickly from E minor into D major, obviously relates back to the one at 7-10 (which modulates from B minor into A major), for the soprano line, after its initial note of 20, and alto line, except for a tied C♯ at the beginning of 22, are exactly like their earlier counterparts transposed down a perfect fifth. The bass, after *its* first note, follows suit with the bass line from before at the lower perfect fifth for two measures and the upper perfect fourth (because of octave displacement) for an additional measure. Then, in place of a continuation of the sequence like the continuation in measure 10, this passage (starting in the middle of of 23) picks up on a freely inverted account of the countersubject material just presented, treating it in the same fashion, with a sequence that has its second stage down a fifth from the first, and third stage up a fourth from the second. As part of this upside-down activity is going on in the bass, the alto and soprano continue their sequential activity with two-bar stages beyond the point where it concludes during the first episode. Suggestions of B minor come about at measure 24 and after, providing some tonal ambivalence prior to its firmer establishment as a key a few measures later, at 29.

Example 15-5.  Measures 20-26

The continuation of this second episode at measures 26-27-28 relates back to the continuation of the first episode at 11-12-13 because of the imitative/sequential treatment involving thirty-second-note portions of the subject's third measure between the same two voices; however, the earlier passage was based upon right-side-up treatment of the configuration comprising the second beat of the subject's third bar, and this later passage exploits *upside-down* treatment (like that given to the countersubject material which precedes it in the bass during measures 23-25) of the configurations comprising the second *and* third beats of the subject's third bar. Interval expansion, which turns second-beat material into third-beat material in the soprano on beat two of 26, allows for continuation of the B-minor triad in arpeggiation, but interval expansion is applied in a different way to the bass material on beat three of 26, causing its imitation of the soprano, which begins at the lower octave now and persists past the second beat, to become free in such a way as to outline the E-minor triad.

Convergence of the two voices in homorhythmic style takes place on beat two of measures 26 and 27 (as opposed to beat *three* of 11 and 12), but both voices are again sequential, the soprano with three one-bar stages (26-27-28) that descend by degree, and the bass with two (the second of which has its first note--the initial A in measure 27--displaced upward by two octaves); therefore, the procedure from before with regard to the number of sequential stages has been reversed. Tying in with this reversal, after the bass's use of inverted material has ended on the first beat of 28, is its two-stage sequence (on the second and third beats) of the right-side-up material found with *three* sequential stages in the *soprano*, starting on beat three of measure 12.

Parallels with earlier structural events come to a halt at measure 29, by which point B minor has returned. Intervalically adjusted statements of the subject's first measure are given out here, first by the soprano, then the alto (which resumes at measure 30 after almost four measures of rest), then by the soprano again, which contributes a Neapolitan-sixth-chord flavor with its C-natural in measure 31, prior to the half cadence of 31-32. This cadence ends on a third-inversion dominant seventh chord, and it has been made especially convincing by its use of a fermata--an unusual occurrence (see Number Six, however) at interior cadence points in the sinfonias, which usually maintain rhythmic momentum from start to finish (Example 15-6).

Example 15-6.   Measures 26-32

During measure 33, where the lower two voices rest, the soprano brings back all but the first note of measure 3, following which in 34, the bass imitates the soprano at the lower tenth as the upper two voices sustain the third and fifth of a submediant chord. Dominant-seventh-of-the-dominant harmony is used during 35, where a modified account of the subject appears in the soprano, and following a resolution to the dominant seventh chord at the beginning of 36, the countersubject fragment originally found in the bass during the last part of measure 1 reappears in all three voices simultaneously, projecting no fewer than five consecutive triads in second inversion. A final fleeting reference to countersubject material (from the third beat of measure 2) is made by the soprano at the beginning of 37, prior to a cadential-six-four pattern which leads into the final cadence.

Example 15-7.   Measures 33-38

**Sinfonia 1.**

142

Sinfonia 4.

Sinfonia 5.

Sinfonia 7.

Sinfonia 8.

Sinfonia 9.

154

158

Sinfonia 13.

162

Sinfonia 14.

INDEX